LLEWELLYN'S
Little Book of
DREAMS

© David LaPorte

Dr. Michael Lennox (Los Angeles, CA) is a practicing psychologist and one of the most respected and sought-after dream interpreters in the US. He has appeared on SyFy, MTV, and many radio shows, and has published articles in *Today's Woman*, *TV Guide*, and other magazines. His previous books include *Dream Sight: A Dictionary and Guide for Interpreting Any Dream* and *Llewellyn's Complete Dictionary of Dreams*. Visit him at www.michaellennox.com.

LLEWELLYN'S
Little Book of

DREAMS

DR. MICHAEL LENNOX

LLEWELLYN PUBLICATIONS
WOODBURY, MINNESOTA

FIRST EDITION
Fourth Printing, 2022

Based on book design by Rebecca Zins
Cover cartouche by Freepik
Cover design by Lisa Novak

Llewellyn's Complete Dictionary of Dreams by Dr. Michael Lennox © 2015
Llewellyn Worldwide Ltd., 2143 Wooddale Drive, Woodbury, MN 55125.
All rights reserved, used by permission.

Llewellyn Publications is a registered trademark of Llewellyn Worldwide Ltd.

Library of Congress Cataloging-in-Publication Data
https://lccn.loc.gov/2017011796

Llewellyn Publications
A Division of Llewellyn Worldwide Ltd.
2143 Wooddale Drive
Woodbury, MN 55125-2989
www.llewellyn.com

Printed in China

Contents

∽

Exercises

INTRODUCTION

My very first childhood memories are dreams. For me, those images are as powerful as waking-life events that occurred during the same time period, if not more so. The most potent one came when I was just three years old. I dreamed of being in this vast space where I was aware of things above me being unfathomably huge and things below me being inconceivably small—a dream I later recognized as symbolically representing the concept of infinity.

The dream was terrifying to me such that I remember it to this day. Years later, I heard this exact same imagery described by someone else, and I felt a sense of coming full circle. From the time I could perceive my own identity, I was connecting through my dreams with the collective unconscious. Though it would be decades before I even knew what that was, dreams would indeed connect me to myself, to others, and to the world around me as a lifelong passion.

It was as a teenager that I discovered my gifts as a dream interpreter. While at summer camp and later in high school, I noticed that my friends and peers were constantly sharing their dreams with each other. It was not uncommon for a conversation to begin with the frequently expressed notion that "I had the craziest dream last night!" We were—as I would later find that most people are—very motivated to share our dreams with each other in social settings. I inserted myself into the mix as someone who could discern the meaning behind these mysterious nighttime phenomena. But to see why I even opened my mouth, we have to go back a few years to my early childhood.

There was always music playing in my home on the weekends. My mother was fond of playing her records (for the under-thirty crowd, those are really big, black CDs), which exposed me to classical music, folk singers, and a smattering of Broadway show scores, one of which was *Fiddler on the Roof*. In *Fiddler*, there is this wonderful sequence in which Tevye tells his wife about a dream he had, and she offers to interpret it. This act of her telling him what his dream means is crucial to the unfolding of the plot. Having heard this recording countless times, I can't express how strongly that idea was imprinted on my brain. The impact of Tevye's dream, and more importantly, Golde's interpretation of it, is a lynchpin on which an important piece of the narrative of the play hinges. Though it was innocuous at the time, listening to this over and over as a child was to be one of the most important experiences of my life.

When I was fifteen, my mother was working toward a master's degree in social work. I had always been captivated by the books on her shelf. One day I spotted Freud's *Interpretation of Dreams*. I pored over it ravenously. As precocious as I was, I don't imagine that I understood any of the material at such a young age, but I definitely gained one very important piece of information from those pages: a dream is something that comes from the inside of a person's mind, and by interpreting it, one can gain some information of value.

So when my teenage friends began to mention their dreams when we were out and about, I found myself unable to stifle the impulse to ask to hear about them and offer something in response. I can't quite imagine what presumptuousness prompted me to make such an outlandish offer, but not being one to hold back my opinions, I did just that. As a result, an amazing thing began to happen. I would listen to the dream and my imagination would ignite. I would then offer some thoughts about what the dream might mean from this imaginative place.

At the time, I had absolutely no idea what I was doing, but from the very start, people responded with curiosity and, more alarmingly, satisfaction. I clearly had a gift and thus began doing this over and over again until, by the time I was in my mid- to late twenties, I had interpreted hundreds of dreams for people. It was not unusual for my phone to ring and the caller to say, "My friend so-and-so tells me that you can tell me what my dream means!" I was hooked.

Over the decades that followed, I continued to dedicate my life and my work to dreams and dream interpretation. I eventually earned a master's and a doctorate degree in psychology. Interestingly, in grad school, the narrative on dreams and their interpretation was very narrow and extremely clear: We were never, ever to interpret a dream for a client. Instead, we were invited to hold space while the client mused about the meaning of their dreams and the images that populated them. But no matter how I tried to take this approach, I could not help the fact that the moment I heard a dream, I intuitively knew its meaning. I continued to have experiences of sharing my perspective with dreamers, almost always to be met with fascination and delight at the insight I offered.

I knew I was doing something very right, and though my approach was discouraged clinically, I vowed to stay true to my gift. But I also decided I needed to figure out what I was doing during this mysterious experience of interpreting dreams so that I could understand it better and perhaps even share my approach with others and teach them to do the same. The first thing I noticed was that dreams are simply stories. They are told in a language of symbols. The symbols have meaning. That meaning is based on the thing itself: what it does, its use or essence, and the qualities it possesses.

A glass holds some drinking water. Water is crucial for life itself. Therefore, the glass of water represents my personal capacity to draw something to me. A broken glass in a dream symbolizes a hampered capacity to attract what I need to function properly.

Every third grader learns that snakes shed their skin. They grow in a way that is not visible to the outside world until, quite suddenly, they are ready to drop their old skin and a new one is complete and ready beneath it. In this way, snakes represent change and transformation. The dream of coming upon a snake while hiking in the woods now has the meaning that change is upon me. My emotional response to the snake—fear or fascination—may color how I am viewing the change in my waking life that is inspiring the dream itself.

Whenever I heard a dream, it was like I was listening to a story. The dreamer would be describing the dream as a narrative, but I found that that wasn't really what I was listening to. It seemed that the language of dreams was symbolic, and it was the symbols that I was actually paying attention to. They lined up in my head in such a way that I heard the story as told to me in this language. The process was something I could understand innately, much like I imagine it would be to be bilingual. The act of me verbalizing an interpretation was me translating the symbols back into a story. What I was translating was a story about the story of the dream itself.

The gift that I have isn't that I know something that other people don't. We all tap into universal meaning through the collective unconscious. My gift is simply that I can do this very, very fast and therefore repeat to the dreamer what I am responding to immediately upon hearing the dream. We all tap into this innate wisdom when we consider our dreams.

It is not necessary to interpret a dream to get value from it. Truly, you don't even need to remember a dream in order for it to be doing all sorts of important things for your mental and physical well-being. Of course, dreams are crazy fun to have and remember, so that's certainly one of the reasons so many people are drawn to them and eager to recall them in detail. Dreams have fascinated humans for thousands of years and doubtless will continue to capture our attention for countless millennia to come.

I have gotten to witness an astonishing number of discoveries about sleeping and dreaming made by scientists in my lifetime. So much has been revealed about the science of sleeping and dreaming that we are closing the gap between what we know and what we don't know by leaps and bounds. And though science and mysticism are still in a battle for supremacy when it comes to understanding dreams, we still don't truly know what dreams are and why we have them. If you're like me, you don't need to know the answers to those questions to find your dreams compelling and want to understand them more deeply. If having a richer, more vibrant experience of your dreams sounds good, then this book is for you.

Chapter One

THE WORLD OF DREAMS: A BRIEF OVERVIEW

The first questions I am always asked about dreams are what are they and why do we have them? Dreams are universal. Everyone has them, even if they don't remember them. We suspect that our animal friends have them as well. Anyone who has been delighted by their dog's shaking leg can attest to this. Our fascination with dreams is understandable, as they are powerful and mysterious. But at the end of the day, when it comes to these fundamental questions of what and why, we simply don't know the answers.

Dreams: In the Beginning

While it is impossible to know exactly how and why humans began to gather together in groups, one could easily imagine the reason for this being connected to fire. Cooperation is the cornerstone of civilization, and at some point roughly forty or fifty thousand years ago, bands of human beings began to come together in a way that was more united than ever before. We began to collaborate while hunting and gathering, and through the spirit of true democracy, we began to thrive—and so was born the idea of community.

Imagine it this way: There is no television, no *Real Housewives of the Serengeti* to keep you entertained. Instead, you find yourself sitting around the fire and you want to share your dream about Grandma, who recently died. You speak of how Grandma visited you while you were sleeping. From across the campfire, someone shouts, "Me too! She also visited me last night." The landscape of the dream world is a place where Grandma, no longer among the living, seems to be available to those who are still around. Suddenly, we see the beginnings not only of what will become known as the collective unconscious, through which all of humanity is connected, but also the notions of ancestors and an afterlife, where we remain in touch with those who have passed over.

Time marches on, and from Mesopotamia to Egypt and then to Greece and Rome, dreams were featured in mythology and poetry and were a major part of all spiritual disciplines. In fact, the original appearance of a religion-based split between good and evil was found in the early civilizations of Babylonia and Assyria. In almost all of these early cultures, dreams were considered to be signs sent directly from the gods. There was a sense that the land to which the dreamer was taken during nighttime narratives was literal; the dreamer would actually leave their body and travel to another dimension where dreams took place. Good dreams were thought to be divine, and bad dreams the result of demonic influences.

These notions evolved into what became modern religious beliefs. The Bible, both the Old and the New Testament, are filled with references to dreams as part of the spiritual life of humans and the way that God speaks to people. The Quran is the same. The Hindu religion has a good deal of reverence for dreams and dream interpretation; however, most symbols are understood to be portents of good and bad events that are likely to befall the dreamer and their loved ones. Though dreams have no place in Buddhism as a practice, even the life of the Buddha himself started with a dream his mother had in which she felt it was prophesied that her child would be a spiritual leader with the whole world as his domain.

You know that dream dictionary you have by the side of your bed? Even those have been around for a while. The very first in history may be one that was unearthed in and preserved from ancient Egypt. Housed in the British Museum and known as the "Dream Book," this document, written on papyrus, divides dreams into good and bad, much like the Babylonian and Assyrian notions that preceded it. This document presents a little over a hundred dream scenarios and just about as many waking-life emotions and behaviors, and offers an interpretation for each.

The Founders of Dream Interpretation

There was a major shift in the interpretation of dreams from a religious to a scientific approach that came with the emergence of psychologists Sigmund Freud and Carl Jung in the mid-nineteenth century. When we consider Freud today, most people think of "Freudian slips" and an obsession with sex. And indeed, Freud was about as sex-obsessed as you can get. By virtue of this, he attributed just about every behavior to this primal drive that makes us human. Freud's heir apparent and student, a younger Swiss psychologist by the name of Carl Gustav Jung, had a bit more to say about where dreams come from and what they are about. This difference in perspective ultimately led to the demise of their collaboration in a fascinating tale of bitterness and rivalry.

Both men were brilliant theorists whose original ideas have so thoroughly entered our day-to-day consciousness that their work has impacted how modern human beings understand our humanity. Very excited about the work Freud was doing, Jung—himself a near-famous up-and-coming young doctor—traveled from Switzerland to Vienna to study with him. Jung was captivated by the idea of dreams being what Freud so aptly called "the royal road to the unconscious." Freud, the elder of the two, thought he had found in Jung the perfect apostle. In fact, both men felt this was the beginning of a life-long association. It was not. In fact, it ended badly. Freud demanded a rigid loyalty from his followers that left absolutely no room for disagreement. Jung was authoritative and opinionated and often brutal in the expression of his opinions. The two didn't mix well.

The role of dreams was central to their discussions. But Freud was utterly obsessed with sex, which permeated all his theories to an extent that is considered almost ridiculous today. Here's an example of Freudian dream interpretation. You dream of climbing stairs: that represents sex. You dream of a mountain: that's a penis. You dream of a cave in the mountain: that's a vagina. There is a train: that's a penis. The train goes through a tunnel: that's intercourse. At the end of the dream, you smoke a cigarette—and, well, we all know what that means.

By all accounts, Jung liked sex just as much as the next person. He knew, however, that there was much more to the story of dreams than that. Freud felt that the sex drive was the only mechanism that inspired human beings. Jung knew instinctively that there were many drives and the human mind was far more sophisticated and interesting. He left Freud and headed back to Switzerland and devoted the rest of his life to figuring it all out.

Over the years, Jung began to treat the local, wealthy neurotics in his own way, and dream interpretation became a foundational pillar of that work. One thing he noticed was that all his patients seemed to have the same dreams. Falling, flying, losing their teeth, and being chased all recurred with alarming regularity, even in his own dreams. When he later traveled to Africa and spent some time with tribal communities, he was astonished to learn that these aboriginal people were having the very same dreams as his white, upper-class Swiss brethren. Everybody was falling, flying, losing their teeth, and being chased. Of course, the Africans were being chased by lions and the Swiss were being chased by bankers or assailants with guns, but the essential content was the same. Jung surmised that there must be some plane of thought that all people share, regardless of where they live, what culture they come from, or how they have been raised. Thus was born his notion of the collective unconscious, which is a major factor in the interpretation of dreams, as you will see.

The Sleeping Brain

Of course, science has come a long way in the century or so that has passed since Freud and Jung popularized the notion of dreams having significant psychological meaning. Ironically, the hubris of the scientific approach has done enormous damage to the mystical appreciation of dreams. As we discover various structures in the brain that participate in dreaming and chemicals that are responsible for sleep, the empirical hubris declares, "And therefore, dreams have no meaning." Of course, anyone who has ever had a powerful dream experience (which is most people) will tell you that the notion that dreams are important and meaningful is simply undeniable, even if they don't know exactly how or why this is true for them.

That being said, I think it is important to be aware of the growing body of knowledge that focuses on the technical side of dreaming. The sleeping brain is filled with fascinating constructs, and science is offering us more details about what is happening inside the brain at a rapid pace. Rather than letting this expanding body of knowledge take away from our appreciation of the mystery of dreaming, we can actually allow it to enhance it.

There are five distinct stages of sleep. Most people are very familiar with REM sleep, or rapid eye movement sleep, where the eyes move rapidly. It is during this stage that typical dreams occur, and in some ways REM is the actual goal of sleep itself. However, there are four other stages of sleep, which are simply numbered in the order in which they occur. From the perspective of the sleeper, there would be very little difference between each of these four partitions of the sleeping experience. They are named based solely on the progression of the waves of energy that can be measured in a sleep lab.

Anyone who has ever had a powerful
dream experience (which is most people)
will tell you that the notion that
dreams are important and meaningful
is simply undeniable,
even if they don't know exactly how
or why this is true for them.

REM sleep is the fifth and final stage of a cycle that repeats itself several times in one night, usually once every ninety minutes or so. We spend somewhere between fifteen and twenty minutes per cycle in REM, and as the night progresses, the amount of time we spend in this segment increases. Though our dreams during REM are particularly vivid, most people tend to remember only the dreams they have upon waking, such that dreams during the middle of the night are generally lost.

In the REM stage, the brain begins to act very much like it does when awake. The same is true for the body, though the limbs are paralyzed, so there is no ability to move about in response to this. The heart rate increases, blood pressure rises, both men and women experience genital engorgement, and the body fluctuates in temperature. In essence, the brain and body act very much like they do when a person is awake, reexperiencing, in many cases, the events of the day. In fact, there is evidence that the brain is indeed revisiting the day's events. If the paralysis that is a natural part of this stage is ineffective, the individual may sleepwalk, talk, or experience night terrors.

But what is the brain really doing during sleep? All the cells in the body—including those in the brain—are like miniature self-contained factories. They are dedicated to a singular purpose at which they excel, and their design and structure are oriented toward whatever that purpose is. Each cell is regulated by a nucleus, a central hub of intelligence that manages all the activity that takes place there and is akin to the executive offices at a manufacturing business. The cells take in and use fuel to create the energy they require to get their job done. And, of course, that process of turning fuel into energy creates waste that must be managed and eliminated—in other words, cell poop.

Your brain has about 100 billion neurons in it. Each neuron is directly connected to about 1,000 individual cells and is capable of firing at a rate of about 200 times per second. That's roughly 20,000,000,000,000,000 bits of information transmitted per second. A single thought or momentary experience gets recorded in the brain in this way in a seemingly infinite crisscrossing web of data, firing up countless cells engaged in powerful activity. This creates a lot of poop to clean up. No wonder the brain needs sleep to rest from this enormous effort!

During sleep, the brain cells actually shrink. At the same time, there is an increase in the amount of cerebrospinal fluid that circulates throughout the brain. This increased volume of liquid, in combination with the added space created by the shrinking cells, is like a faucet being turned on.

Then, as the cells return to their normal size, the excess amount of waste products from brain-cell activity is flushed out. This helps explain why, after a bad night's sleep, we tend to feel foggy and cognitively impaired. Long-term sleep deprivation can be harmful or even fatal, and the culprit ultimately is the waste product of brain cells converting fuel into energy.

Another primary action being attended to during REM sleep is the formation of memory. As we go about our lives, we see, hear, touch, and experience all sorts of events. Our sensory receptors collect this data and send it to the brain, which in turn converts these stimuli into electrical impulses that record the data. Each sight, sound, or interaction with the world is stored as a path of countless neurons rapidly firing in a string, in the same way that a digital recorder "hears" sound and immediately converts it into a pattern of ones and zeros.

Then in REM sleep we are essentially reexperiencing the same stimulation and reliving the events that were recorded during the day. Remember that the waking alertness of the brain looks pretty much the same as the activity of REM sleep. This is where the events of the day are being reactivated, ostensibly for permanent recording in other areas of the brain where short-term memory is made, stored, and eventually turned into the permanent record of our life unfolding, event to event, as part of our long-term memory.

And what is it that we are left with at the end of the day? Are dreams random, meaningless events based on the chaos of the brain, or are they deep, profound messages from the unconscious mind? Do they connect us to the mysterious realm that exists just beyond the veil of reality where our ancestors dwell, or are they just fodder for interesting tales told around the fires of the ancient world or the modern-day office water cooler? Do dreams connect us to the power of the collective unconscious, or do they tell us more about our repressed sexual desires? Truly, none of this matters, because if you picked up this book, you are like the millions of people who know from personal experience that the significance of their dreams is undeniable because of how meaningful they feel.

Many a time I have suffered
a sort of dream envy over people
who find themselves in wildly fantastical
landscapes and mind-bending narratives.
And yet there are those who dream
so often of their workplace that they
can't seem to escape their office,
even in their sleep.

Chapter Two

TYPES OF DREAMS

Dreams come in an endless variety of styles and types. Even dreamers have an individual personality; many people consistently dream in particular themes, images, and structures. I, myself, am a very mundane dreamer. Of course, just like everyone, anything can happen in my dreams and probably will. But since I have had the benefit of hearing dozens of dreams in a fairly constant stream for decades now, there is much for me to compare mine to. Many a time I have suffered a sort of dream envy over people who find themselves in wildly fantastical landscapes and mind-bending narratives. And yet there are those who dream so often of their workplace that they can't seem to escape their office, even in their sleep.

There are, however, certain very specific types of dreams and sleep experiences that most dreams fall into, so if you want to begin an exploration of the world of dreaming, it can be very helpful to start here. Additionally, some dream types perform very specific functions, and it can be beneficial to know if a dream you had falls into one of these categories. Lastly, there are phenomena that show up through dreams that always inspire questions when I am out in the world teaching, so some of this chapter is devoted to those experiences.

Nightmares

Unfortunately, the age-old question of why we have nightmares has no answer. From a scientific perspective, we have no idea why in some dreams we find ourselves in terrifying landscapes where horrific things occur. Children tend to have many more nightmares than adults, and most eventually grow out of this. That being said, no one is ever nightmare-free, and deeply disturbing dreams, some of which can jolt a person awake, are a natural part of the dreaming experience.

There may be some sleep-stage and brain-structure components that actually contribute directly to nightmares, but we don't know enough scientifically to say how this might work. We do know that we are more likely to have nightmares toward the end of a night of sleep, when the REM cycle is the longest. Additionally, the amygdala—a structure at the very center of the brain related to the regulation of powerful emotions—is also more active during a nightmare experience. There may be neurochemical factors involved in nightmares that we just aren't sophisticated enough to understand.

There are a number of theoretical causes of nightmares that are largely agreed upon in the world of psychology. One, which will be touched upon in the recurring dream section later in this chapter, is that a nightmare is simply a response to stress. Whether a nightmare is a recurring image or a one-off original, the majority of such nocturnal phenomena seem to be related to working out stress, fears, and anxieties from waking life.

A staple in media is the dream-related past-abuse model, which, while a wonderful dramatic device used in storytelling in film and television, is a much rarer phenomenon in

Whether a nightmare is a recurring image
or a one-off original,
the majority of such nocturnal phenomena
seem to be related to
working out stress, fears,
and anxieties from waking life.

real-life dream experiences outside of cases of post-traumatic stress syndrome. Of course, it does happen that some individuals suppress traumatic events and emotional disturbances from early life that then show up in the dream state in the form of nightmares. As an example, a young woman who suffered from sexual abuse within her family of origin reported a nightmare of looking down upon a valley filled with houses late at night. Inside each of the houses she knew there were people having sex. Though there was no real danger present in the dream content, she found the dream very disturbing and she woke up feeling great anxiety. In the interpretation of this dream, each house represented the dreamer's desire to compartmentalize her experience of her own sexuality, which didn't feel like a safe mode of expression because of her wounded past. This dream helped lead the dreamer into some exploration of the past abuse and her ability to heal.

It is likely that the reason why the question about what causes nightmares is so ubiquitous is because of our desire to be free of them. We tend to believe that if we know what causes an unwanted thing, we might be able to eradicate it from our experience. However, the very consistency of nightmares, whatever their cause, implies that they are a necessity. And though we may never know exactly why nightmares happen, they are probably tied to something important about the fitness of our mind and the psychic equilibrium we need to function effectively in our waking life.

Compensatory Dreams

Most of the dreams we have fall in this category. Compensatory comes from the word *compensate*. When a thing compensates, it is making up for something that is missing, or trading one thing for another. Like being paid for a job that you do, this is really about balancing out a situation and creating stasis. Dreams help make up for emotional and psychic inequities in our daily waking lives. Freud called this "wish fulfillment" and believed that most dreams were doing just that: fulfilling wishes about life that are buried in the unconscious.

The human psyche craves balance; in fact, all of life seems designed to harmonize in this way. As one energy moves in a particular direction, its counterbalance immediately moves in tandem so that equilibrium is the result. Biology and physics are filled with examples of this concept in action, from osmosis to the law of inertia, where a moving body will eventually come to rest because of the intervention of outside forces. The human psyche is like this as well, and dreaming itself is designed to perform this task. Dreams help us assimilate new information that we are attempting to learn, whether that information is about the algebra we are going to be tested on in math class or the mysteries of how to be a better person. This occurs unconsciously, whether we remember our dreams or not.

Each time we sleep deeply enough to dream, we are enacting experiences that help us process the information that we are being bombarded with during the day. Because the language of dreams is symbolic and not literal, it is usually not clear, initially, what is being addressed. This is one of the reasons why dream interpretation can be so valuable. Life is a constant series of confrontations with experiences that not only are challenging in and of themselves but also tap into the memories of earlier wounds and hurts that we carry with us along the way. By confronting and expressing our deepest fears, secret desires, and debilitating challenges within the safe confines of the dream state, we are able to wake up and return to our daily lives feeling restored to balance. In fact, sometimes the dream world offers us a forum in which to process difficult emotions such as rage or grief, which would be impossible to do in our daily lives without experiencing a debilitating level of confrontation or embarrassment.

The magical nature of dreams can also allow the dreamer to attain impossible desires that can relieve certain tensions, much in the same way that scratching can cause the sensation of an itch to disappear. When Freud coined the term "wish fulfillment," he was referring to the idea that dreams can often satisfy the need to realize a longing or desire so that you can awake feeling complete and not see your life as missing something that is not present. Though some dreams are obviously this type, it is possible that all dreams actually fall in this category.

Not every compensatory dream has a desirable outcome. Dreaming of having sex with a beautiful movie star might represent a wish fulfilled, but it also might be compensating for an underlying lack in the dreamer's self-esteem or perceived level of attractiveness. Also, *desirable* may not always be synonymous with *constructive*. Say, for example, a man has frequent dreams of murdering his detested neighbor. On the face of it, this could appear to be a wish fulfillment dream in which the man gets rid of the source of his frustration. However, the real purpose of the dream may be to help the dreamer process his anger in such a way that he is better equipped to wake up the following morning and not feel the need to act out his feelings because he already did so in his dreams.

Recurring Dreams: Anxiety-Based

Recurring dreams are not necessarily the most common type of dreams that people have, but they are the ones that are most readily remembered and frequently talked about. This is likely because the fact that they recur keeps them in the forefront of the dreamer's mind. And this is, of course, what the underlying purpose of a recurring dream actually is. If a dream comes again and again, it is attempting to do something very specific. It is trying to get your attention.

There are two very distinct categories of recurring dreams. While both appear to fit under the same general heading of "recurring" (that is, they recur), they are actually very different styles of dreaming that have completely different functions. The more ubiquitous of these types of dreams are the ones related to anxiety.

Stress is a constant companion to most of us in the modern world and is often misinterpreted as an actual tool for getting through life. Presented with obligations and obstacles, many of us have grown to believe that it is the stress itself that helps us meet those obligations and overcome those obstacles. This is, of course, a great misconception, and research shows that stress can be quite detrimental to both physical and mental health.

There are all kinds of beneficial and scientifically proven stress combatants, from exercise and meditation to medication, proper nutrition, and more. However, there is one prominent, organic tool for reducing stress that is built into the human mechanism and is without a doubt the most effective one there is: dreaming.

The stress we experience throughout life will fluctuate. Varied circumstances, times in life that bring up issues based on age, and confrontations that depend on the areas of life that are causing anxiety will differ greatly. What will not always be different, however, is the way in which the unconscious mind uses dreams to regulate that stress and reduce it to a non-lethal level, allowing us to wake up each morning and do it all over again.

Because the human mind is economical, it will often turn to a recognizable image that has worked in the past to convey certain emotional states. We experience this in the form of recurring dreams. These are those pervasive dreams that trouble us from time to time, such as the ones in which we are being chased, or are falling, or are naked in public, to name a few common ones. These dreams usually are not filled with elaborate plots and characterizations, but are rather simplistic, with a familiar theme.

A person who regularly dreams of being chased will likely not have much detail beyond the act of running from an enemy, often unknown to them. The enemy is remembered as frightening and usually leaves the dreamer with residual anxiety. This common dream serves an important purpose when our waking life presents us with scary life experiences. A person who is under great stress might experience this dream image in order to process the unconscious fears that come up as the result of chaos in their life. Their ability to survive the danger or panic present in the dream may actually be helping them navigate their daytime obstacles. It is living out the raw blast of unbridled fear in their dreams that allows them to wake up feeling a sense of balance and not emotionally ragged.

The dream of returning unprepared to a high school setting also falls in this category. This type of dream will often recur when a person is not feeling ready or prepared for whatever life is presenting. At a moment when their ability to perform is under scrutiny, a person might dream of being back in high school and unprepared for a test. Any dream that points out this sort of vulnerability is helping the person to balance out underlying feelings of inadequacy or insecurity.

Other anxiety-based dreams include teeth falling out, feeling lost, being under attack, tsunamis, falling, etc. There are so many versions of these that it would be impossible to mention them all. They are connected to underlying feelings of fear. Since these themes commonly recur in life, they commonly recur in dreams.

Almost everyone has a specific image that they can point to as being a frequent dream, often beginning in childhood. As an example, say you are someone who has a recurring dream of driving a car up a steep hill. You keep going, only to get to a point where you are on such a steep incline that your car can no longer move forward and begins to slide backward. The feeling is terrifying as you completely lose control of the car as it careens backward. You are left feeling panicked and useless as you plummet to what is certain death. And then, of course, you wake up.

You dream this dream frequently and have done so for years. This is simply a function of your mind's dynamic response to this particular image. It is perfectly suited to accurately express the various stresses of your individual life. It hardly matters what it is in your waking life that is inspiring the dream. An argument with a friend or a large credit card bill that you are worried about paying on time could both elicit the very same dream. Both waking-life circumstances are clearly very different in nature, but the dream that helps you restore your psychic balance is the same.

Recurring Dreams: Process-Based

This type of recurring dream is very different from the anxiety-based ones just described. These dreams are considered recurring because the individual dreams, though they may vary in certain ways, feature repeated themes and sometimes developing stories where each dream builds somehow on the previous dream. In fact, a series of dreams that occur over a period of a week or more can be alarming with regard to the information they reveal.

Dreams of this nature are often scary. What makes them process-based as opposed to anxiety-based is this: Anxiety-based dreams have a very simple function. They take elements of waking life that are causing stress and help the dreamer's mind lessen the stress and anxiety, so that life can be faced a bit freer of that debilitating human challenge, the anxious mind. Process-based dreams are specifically aligned with a change or transformation a person is going through that is particular to a set of life circumstances or a series of events that are confronting or challenging. The "process" that is being described here is the process of growing, expanding consciousness, and changing from the inside out.

The continuity of these dreams can vary, from a few times in a short period to repeatedly over many years. Usually more elaborate, they tend to involve images particular to the dreamer's life experience. These more personalized dreams usually connect to a specific emotional wound that may be being healed through the dream world. The distinction with this type of dream is that it will relate specifically to the issue being expressed. This type of dream may change slightly with each recurrence and will continue until the process completes itself.

One example that should be recognized as fairly common connects to how dream work can help us to process loss and grief. When we lose someone through death or the end of a relationship, we often continually dream of that person in a way that reflects the gradual letting go that accompanies such a separation. The dream may recur until the process of separation feels complete. Each dream may be thematically similar, with shifting elements that embody the change taking place. Each progressive dream may feature less and less proximity to the person

Anxiety-based dreams
have a very simple function.
They take elements of waking life
that are causing stress
and help the dreamer's mind
lessen the stress and anxiety,
so that life can be faced
a bit freer of that debilitating
human challenge,
the anxious mind.

being dreamed about. This reflects the arc of the grief process, and the dreams will likely stop when that process is complete.

Any dramatic life change can be expressed through a series of recurring dream images. A woman in her thirties who moved away from home after a divorce reported having recurring dreams about cars after driving across the country to her new life. Each successive dream reflected her then-current relationship to this life change by virtue of the condition and type of car that appeared in her dreams. The more smoothly her waking life seemed to be going, the better functioning the car appeared to be. She could literally chart her own emotional development according to the condition of the cars in her dreams.

Another example is a writer in her late twenties who was having a recurring nightmare of being pregnant and murdering her newborn child. In each successive dream, she carried the baby to term, only to kill the child after giving birth. In the first of these nightmares, she strangled the baby and woke up in a panic. Every week or so, the dream returned and became more and more gruesome and bloody in its imagery.

The woman was horrified by this series of recurring nightmares and sought help to understand what they might mean. Once she was introduced to the symbolic meaning of babies as new directions in life, she was able to connect the fearful dreams with the numerous first drafts of a creative project she was trying to get off the ground. The dreams were expressing her trial-and-error approach and the frustration of having to kill off the creative impulses that didn't feel right and making space to birth something better. Once seen in this light, the dreams lost their frightening hold over her and the nightmares immediately stopped.

People engaged in a recovery process from any sort of addiction may experience a particular brand of process-based recurring dream that is also compensatory in nature. It is quite common for members of twelve-step groups to have dreams of slipping back into their destructive behavior. Addictive behavior serves the purpose of creating an emotional buffer from life's difficulties. When a daytime experience challenges the emotional vulnerability of such a person, they may counteract overwhelming feelings by dreaming of their old form of escape. It may be the very thing that allows them to face their fears without relinquishing their success in sobriety. While these dreams are often accompanied by a level of regret as intense as if the person had actually fallen off the wagon in real life, these dreams usually subside as the person continues to stay clean and sober.

Here's a recurring dream from a man in his mid-forties who was faced with the prospect of completing a very big work project that was designed to lead to a fairly significant career enhancement. The project represented two levels of stress, the first being the work itself and the second connecting to the added level of responsibility that being successful with the project would lead to. Several days into a crisis of feeling unable to attend to the project with the diligence it required, the man described recurring dreams of having to climb Mount Kilimanjaro in three days' time with his family of origin. In the dreams, he was overwhelmed by the task itself, but he was also excited at the prospect of facing the unknown dangers and experiencing what it would be like to reach the summit.

This dream was clearly connected to unconscious feelings of resistance to the hard work that his life was requiring of him. Climbing the mountain in the dreams was the symbolic climb that it sometimes feels like we're making in real life, especially when we're faced with a specific task that feels daunting. Because the man's family of origin was part of these dreams, he knew that he was considering his entire life and not just this small moment

in time. By working with this dream series in a very dili-
gent manner, the dreamer once again found his discipline
increase and his focus sharpen. And just as valuable, he
was able to connect deeply and authentically to his feelings of fear, vulnerability, and utter terror at the prospect
of failing.

Precognitive Dreams

Intuitive phenomena come in many different forms, but
they all have one thing in common: the use or expression of what is sometimes called the "sixth sense." This
is a way of synthesizing information that is not derived
from the five generally accepted senses of sight, touch,
smell, taste, and hearing. People with this facility in abundance are sometimes called psychic or clairvoyant, and
this innately human ability is often referred to as instincts
or street smarts. No matter what you call it, all human
beings are intuitive to some extent.

Intuition can be accessed without any distractions or
doubtful second-guessing by people in their dreams. Some
connect so easily to their sixth sense in this way that, on
occasion, they report having dreams that contain information about events that have yet to occur. This is called precognitive dreaming.

Some people claim
to see future events
in their dreams
and also to experience
dreamlike visitations from
people who have just died,
without their knowing
that the person in question
had indeed passed away.

There are two general types of precognitive dreaming. The first and most commonly occurring type is when a person has a dream in which the scenario and sometimes the events of the dream seem to occur in the dreamer's waking life anywhere from days to weeks or even years following the dream. Such an experience is usually not recognized as a precognitive dream at the time of the dream. Only later, when the event actually occurs, does the dreamer recollect the scenario from the previous dream.

For example, a person is grocery shopping. They pass another shopper and bump shopping carts. They suddenly remember, perhaps quite unexpectedly, that they recently dreamed of just such an interaction, shopping cart and all. It is hard to identify if this type of experience is an actual psychic phenomenon or just a trick of a vivid imagination, but it certainly is an experience described by many people from all walks of life.

Some people claim to see future events in their dreams and also to experience dreamlike visitations from people who have just died, without their knowing that the person in question had indeed passed away. One example about a future event was described by a woman who claimed to have had precognitive dreams her entire life. She dreamed of her sister having a car accident while driving in a blue car in the rain. Indeed, several months later, her sister crashed into a railing during a rainstorm in her new blue car.

What is important to know about precognitive dreams is that most people who have them are well aware that they will periodically have such a dream. A person who has never had such a dream before may be terrified after having a dream in which they, for example, witness the death of a loved one. They will sometimes immediately assume that their friend is doomed, but that is unlikely. Unless this is something that you have a lifetime of experience with, such a dream is far more likely to be a random nightmare than a vision from the invisible world of psychic phenomena.

Visitation Dreams

In the section about the history of dreaming in chapter 1, we discussed the impact of early humans around the globe gathering together and sharing their dreams at the community level. One of the staples of such dream experiences was the appearance of ancestors in the dream landscapes of those still living. Here, we find the very first platform on which the idea of an afterlife was built.

The phenomenon of connecting with loved ones who are deceased is still very much a part of the human experience today. It is common for people to report that after someone close to them has passed away, they experience a dream that feels more like a visitation than a typical dream. Such experiences can be vivid and powerful enough to actually make a person a believer about such things. Here is an example.

It was so hard for me when my mom died. We were very close and she died pretty young. I was twenty-eight. We weren't a religious family, and frankly the idea of whether there is a God or a heaven had never really occurred to me. But something happened when she passed away that completely changed my perspective on the idea of there being a separation between life and death. I dreamed I was in my bed and my mother came into the room, sat down on the bed next to me, and put her hand on my hand. It felt real, so much so that when I immediately woke up alone in my room, I was surprised that she wasn't actually there. Of course she wasn't— she was across the county in the hospital. When the phone rang a few minutes later, I was filled with a sense of dread. This was "the" call. My mom had died that night. I didn't tell anyone about this experience because I felt a little crazy, like I must have made it up. I don't know what I believe, really. But I definitely believe that my mom came to me that night for real.

There are definite commonalities to all visitation-style dreams that set them apart from the typical chaotic storytelling variety. First, the setting is always singular. Often taking place in the very room in which the dreamer is sleeping, visitation dreams do not travel from place to place, crossing the boundaries of time and space. Second, the person who is visiting rarely does anything of significance. In fact, they often are simply present, still, and quiet. If they do speak, it is typically a very simple expression that they offer, something to the effect that they are well, that they are at peace, or that they want to communicate their love for the dreamer.

These dreams can be very uplifting and often are reported to play a significant part in the grieving process. It is unfortunate, then, that they do not occur for everyone. Oftentimes, the deeply loved person does not make a nocturnal appearance to the individual who is painfully grieving their loss. There is a widely held view in New Age circles that such visitations occur only when there is some deeper need for such a connection to be made, as if there is some unfinished business to attend to.

Lucid Dreaming

Lucid dreaming is a general term that refers to any number of dream experiences that feature an extra sense of conscious perception while in the dream state. Sometimes it is as simple as becoming aware (as part of the actual content of the dream itself) that you are dreaming. This can appear as a fleeting thought or in a more significant paradigm that pervades the dream landscape. While we currently do not have the ability to understand the phenomenon of lucid dreaming from a scientific perspective, it has certainly been reported by enough dreamers to be considered a bona-fide dreaming experience.

A second type of lucid dreaming that is more active than the one just described involves the ability to influence movement within the dream landscape. First, the dreamer becomes aware that they are dreaming. Second, the viewpoint of the dreamer begins to move, with a powerful sense of direction. The dreamer is then able to choose the direction that this movement takes.

Taken to its most extreme expression, a lucid dream can become quite vivid and literal. Not only can a dreamer recognize that the experience they are currently having is a dream, but this awareness can be cultivated and expanded. A sense of creative power can enter this landscape, and the dream state itself can be elaborated upon and deepened with respect to its capacity to heal psychic wounds, expand psychological self-awareness, and offer guidance from the intuitive elements of the human experience.

Lucid dreaming can directly impact the quality of a person's waking life. One woman who has been lucid dreaming since childhood put it this way: "It's like being out of control in a car and being frightened, but then I say to myself, 'Oh, I'm dreaming,' and I'm no longer afraid. This then applies to my waking life as a result, where I can essentially say the same thing to myself when faced with a difficult situation."

There are many people who are naturally predisposed to having lucid dreams. Most will say that this experience started early in life. One dreamer, now in her early fifties, claims to have had her first vivid and lucid dream experiences as early as five years old. She frequently had a scary recurring dream that took place on the very long driveway that led to her home in a rural part of the United States. In the dream, a van approaches and some kidnappers jump out, clearly meaning to take her by force. She describes suddenly becoming aware that not only is she in a dream, but her very survival in this dream demands that she be somewhere else. She looks down at her hand and sees the ring on her finger that was a gift from her grandmother. Instinctively she knows that if she turns this ring, she can go anywhere she wants. With a touch of the ring, she is transported to Disneyland and is safe from danger.

This example touches on a technique that most teachers of this discipline describe as essential if you are looking to enhance your experience. It involves looking at your hands in the dream state as a trigger to cause you to recognize that you are, in fact, dreaming. In order for this to be effective, it needs to start as a waking-life intention-setting mechanism.

One young man described touching his thumbs to his palms frequently throughout the course of the day, for days on end, as a grounding physical suggestion for the intention to become lucid within the dream state. Sure enough, eventually he did this during a dream, only, because it was a dream, his thumbs went all the way through his palms in a hyper-realistic fashion that alarmed him and alerted him to the fact that he was not awake but had, in effect, woken up inside of his dream. The dream actually continued in this way as he met up with two other young men and convinced them both to recognize that they were dreaming as well. Once his dream compatriots joined him in this exciting experience, they proceeded to manipulate the realities of the construct such that his two-seater car was magically able to accommodate the three of them. They hopped into his car to explore the landscape more extensively.

The need to practice mindfulness and meditation in order to develop the capacity for lucid dreaming cannot be overstated. Maintaining a quiet, open mind during waking hours will increase your ability to bring that same mindfulness into the dreaming state. Setting the intention to have a lucid dream is crucial; consistent and constant thoughtful attention to this desire during the course of the day will have a great impact on the likelihood of success. Creating a specific visual trigger, such as the ring or the hands in the previous examples, is also an important tool to utilize when attempting to increase the potential for lucid dreaming.

The need to practice
mindfulness and meditation
in order to develop
the capacity for lucid dreaming
cannot be overstated.
Maintaining a quiet,
open mind during waking hours
will increase your ability
to bring that same mindfulness
into the dreaming state.

Shared Dreaming

There is a phenomenon in the dreaming world that is somewhat rare but absolutely does occur. The experience of shared dreams, where two people have the same dream at the same time, may sound like something out of a movie. However, this can and does happen. The two people in question usually have to be very close and share a powerful connection. And even though the details of the shared dreams may not be exactly the same (unlike in the movies), the fact remains that reports of such experiences exist.

There is no scientific explanation for a shared dream, of course, but people who have experienced it don't need empirical evidence to validate what happened to them. Certainly, the mysteries of the intuitive mind and the psychic connection that many people tap into have a natural place in the world of dreams. What follows are a few examples from individuals who claim to have shared dreams with others.

> I was fourteen years old and my sister was thirteen when she and I had the same exact dream the night after our mother passed away. In the dream, my mother was hiding behind our bedroom door.

I kept calling out to her to come out fully so that I could see her, but she refused. Then I started to pester her some more, but she would only show half of her face and body, while the rest was hidden behind the door. Her face was very serious and sad and casted over with a shadow, so I began to get a little freaked out. Then I woke up. At breakfast, I kept this to myself, but then my sister said she'd had a dream with Mama and I told her, "Me too!" When I told her mine, she got really quiet and said, "I had the same exact dream."

This particular example illustrates the power of the family connection that is often part of the shared dream experience. Additionally, it seems logical that since the reasons why we dream and the existence of an afterlife are both complete mysteries, perhaps these two phenomena are more related to each other than we have the capacity to explain at our current level of understanding. In this way, the existence of an energetic connection between a recently deceased mother and both of her daughters in the same dream at the same time actually makes sense.

Intimate romantic relationships often allow for such an intuitive connection to exist between two people. In one rather remarkable case, a woman now in her fifties reports that a significant relationship from earlier in her life first appeared in a dream. She dreamed of this man shortly before she met him in life, and in the dream she told him point blank that they were not going to be together. When she met the man in real life, she began a relationship with him that, though difficult and challenging, lasted for several years.

Over the course of their time together, there were several occurrences of shared dreams, especially when they slept in the same bed. Though there were many such experiences, the one that remains most clearly in the woman's memory happened fairly early in their relationship. She dreamed that she was walking to meet a friend of hers and all sorts of crazy things began to happen and scary things began to appear, including monsters and other frightening dreamscape manifestations. In the dream, she called out for her boyfriend, who came to help her. Together they battled the monsters made of light, and after defeating them in some rather scary combat, they went off to go meet the friend.

The next morning, the woman's boyfriend told her about a dream he'd had that very same night. Without having any knowledge of the content of her dream, he told her how he'd dreamed that she was in trouble. In his dream, he heard her calling desperately for him to go and help her, which he did. This sort of shared dream was a constant feature of their dreaming experience. Even their breakup occurred first in the dream world before manifesting in their waking lives.

The final example of a shared dream is one between best friends and is an example of the power of intuition and the perception of subtle energies, and how this mysterious human capacity can be felt in both the dreaming landscape and the waking life. Though this sounds like something out of a movie, it was reported by both of the participants who experienced it. One of them recounted it like this:

A friend and I had a very strange experience that involved having the same dream at the same time, which also turned out to be one of the most important turning points of my life. But to really tell the story, I have to go back to my childhood. My family life provided a strange sort of dichotomy. On the one hand, I was exposed to spiritual principles very early on and spent much of my adolescence studying the power of prayer and affirmation and was introduced to the notion that we create our own reality according to how we are perceiving it. On the other hand, I experienced a level of abuse and neglect that was pretty nightmarish. By the time I was in my early thirties, I had renounced all my spiritual sensibilities. In fact, I was mad at God, mad at the world. I no longer had access to my spiritual sensibility and had really fallen into a victim mentality because of everything that had happened to me.

My friend and I went away for a long weekend to a beautiful cabin in the woods. We both needed a break. Her father had just died and mine was very sick. I have always had a gift for perceiving energy, and as lovely as this cabin was, there was something about it that felt dark and not quite right. Feeling silly, I said nothing to my friend, though the feeling wouldn't go away. At some point that weekend, we decided to curl up for a nap together—I was so relieved that she wanted to sleep together because frankly (though it still felt silly) I didn't want to sleep by myself. After sleeping for forty-five minutes, we both woke up screaming and shaking.

As it turned out, we both had been dreaming almost the same thing. Both of us had dreamt that something terrible and dangerous was coming to get us. For her, it was two men. In my dream, it was much more energetic, like a menacing, dark force. She saw the heads of baby dolls that had been severed and mutilated. In my dream, there were murdered babies. Though the details were different, the feelings we described seemed exactly the same. And, as it turned out, both of us had been having the same negative feelings about the cabin and, feeling pretty silly about it, hadn't said anything to the other. But by then we agreed that no matter what, it was time to go, so we packed our things and left immediately.

That experience was an absolute turning point for me. I immediately began to address the childhood wounds that had been trying so hard to get my attention. I got back onto my spiritual path. And though the healing I needed took some time, I have arrived at a place in my life now where my faith is strong and I no longer see myself as a victim of the things perpetrated upon me in my childhood. My friend and I never did find out anything

about that cabin in the woods, but I know that my
life took an amazing and important turn that weekend and nothing has been the same since.

Though there are far fewer examples of shared dreams
than other types of dreaming, it is something that does
occur. The veil between what is known and what is not
known is thinner than what meets the eye.

Night Terrors

The scientific names for these quite terrifying dream experiences are hypnagogic or hypnopompic hallucinations. The
root word *hypno* comes to us from the Greek god Hyp-
nos, whose domain was sleep itself. Hypnagogic refers to
anything that happens just as sleep is beginning, and hypnopompic relates to the process of waking up out of sleep.
These aptly named night terrors are more likely to happen
in children. They also tend to occur in certain people regularly, while sparing the rest of the population. That said, it
is not uncommon to find that just about everyone has had
at least one experience of waking up terrified and unable
to move.

As we learned in the section about the brain and sleep
in chapter 1, the body is paralyzed during REM sleep.

This is to protect the dreamer from acting out all of the stimulation that the frontal cortex experiences while it reviews the events of the day. If the body was not paralyzed during this important process, the body would naturally respond to all of that stimuli by moving around. For the body's own protection, the muscles related to movement are temporarily shut off.

The thinking mind, the part of the mind that is alert and aware while we are awake, is inactive during all of the stages of sleep. The mechanisms that regulate this complex process make all of the changes—the switching off and on of various systems—happen in a particular order and in a specific way. Sometimes these overlapping states are not as rigidly enforced, and the resulting blurring of boundaries between them can have significant consequences. One of these is night terrors.

The primary cause of a night terror is the partial consciousness of the waking mind that is normally completely shut off during sleep. The part of your mind that holds your identity and orientation to time and space— knowing who you are, what room you are in, and what day/night it is—comes into a state of just enough alertness to be aware of your experience. It is the overlapping of these two modalities of perception that creates the imagery that a night terror generally features.

What is fascinating about these states is the simultaneous experience of what we might call the dreaming mind and conscious awareness. The dreaming mind is multidimensional and irrational. Though it remains a complete mystery, it is certainly dynamic, creative, and expansive. Our conscious awareness is the complete opposite, with limits, boundaries, and a sense of form. The power of the latter is that it is what holds our sense of identity. When that is combined with the infinite nature of the dreaming mind, we are open to perceiving all sorts of subtle energies that, depending upon your belief system, may actually be present and with us at all times. These energies have their root in other dimensions—dimensions that we can reach only in the dream state.

The challenge with this state comes from the paralysis element. The conscious mind is aware that it cannot move, and that sensation often expands to a sense that one cannot breathe, as if something is sitting on one's chest. This is, of course, terrifying indeed. It is arguable that the perceptive state that is opened up because of the presence of the dreaming mind may be just wonderfully expansive and that it is the collapse of the simultaneous sensation of paralysis that makes such a state become an experience of terror.

Sleepwalking and Sleep-Talking

The phenomenon of walking and/or talking during sleep is a result of the release of the paralysis that is ordinarily in place during REM sleep. The brain's activities, therefore, are more freely acted out by the dreamer, and the person may mumble, talk, and move about in the sleeping space. Though this experience can be dangerous, for the most part it is harmless, and the sleeping individual will likely awaken before any real harm is done.

Some dreams are just begging to be worked with and interpreted. Others have less to offer you and might just as well be left as a passing experience in your day-to-day flow of life. The more you consider your dreams, the more clearly you will feel when a dream wants your attention. By understanding some of the types of dream experiences that are common to all people, you should have a better notion of what dreams have value to be explored more deeply. The next chapter will offer you a number of ways to do this work in simple and profound ways.

Chapter Three

WORKING WITH YOUR DREAMS

The most important thing to know about working with your dreams is that there is no wrong way to do this. In fact, dreams don't really need our help at all to provide the service they do for us. Our consciousness is growing every day when we sleep no matter what. You've heard the phrase "Why don't you sleep on it?" Well, this is for very good reason. In sleep, we become better at being human beings. When faced with a decision, great or small, we do in fact know ourselves better with each night we sleep. When we let ourselves sleep on it, we are honoring a profound process that knits together our experience in a constant and expansive weaving of the tapestry of our lives.

Preparing the Way

In the first chapter, I mentioned the notion that through dreaming and the REM sleep cycle, the brain formulates short-term memory. We get smarter in dreams. You might say that we get wiser as well, and that's where the mystical element comes in. On the face of it, smarter and wiser may seem like the same concepts, but I don't think they are. How smart you are could be thought of as the information you know and understand. Wisdom incorporates the ability to synthesize what you know into better and better decisions that lead, over time, to a more satisfying life.

If dreams do not need our help, then what could the value of working with them possibly be? Perhaps it is in the acceleration that occurs when we focus on something we desire. That which we pay attention to tends to magnify and expand. This is true whether we are focusing on fear and doubt or the possibilities of self-awareness and an expansion of consciousness.

Your dreams are happening inside of you, which is an amazing concept when you stop to think about it. You have, at the very center of your being, this wealth of imagination and possibilities and an extraordinary capacity to create magnificent landscapes. In dreams, anything can happen and probably will.

The Hierarchy of Dream Work

Like most things in life, the more you put into your dream work, the more you will get out of it. There are five different steps or levels of working with a dream, each one slightly more beneficial than the one that precedes it:

STEP ONE: Remembering a dream at all brings it into consciousness, thereby elevating the value it can offer in the search for personal understanding.

STEP TWO: Writing your dream down will reinforce the impact of your effort and also lock the memory of your dream in your conscious mind.

STEP THREE: Thinking about and processing the information your dream presents by ruminating on it will deepen the experience.

STEP FOUR: Discussing your dream with another person is going one step further, as an objective viewpoint will always help you see something that you would be unable to see on your own.

STEP FIVE: Responding to your dream with a creative endeavor, such as drawing or writing a poem, takes this process to its highest level of effectiveness. The unconscious mind expresses itself through creative means, and this kind of dream work is the most powerful there is.

It is not necessary to work with every bit of a dream. Whatever fragments you remember or choose to work with will always lead you to the perfect level of insight that you are currently ready to examine. Feeling frustrated or doubtful of your accuracy only undermines your sense of well-being and is in opposition to the way in which unconscious material becomes conscious. There is no right or correct interpretation; there is just the value of leaning into the mystery of the dream imagery.

Do not overcomplicate the process. Go slowly if necessary. Be open-minded. Be patient with your dreams and, most of all, be patient with yourself. And remember, how you interpret a dream becomes part of the process itself. The scenes you remember, the words you use to describe them, and the way you choose to work with them are both significant and revealing.

Writing Down Your Dreams

If you want to be serious about working with your dreams, you have to be willing to write them down. Every person's capacity for remembering their dreams is different. Some can recall all of them down to the smallest detail, whereas others never remember any of their dreams. Most people fall somewhere in between, and it is common to go through different phases where sometimes you remember a lot of them and other times very few.

Wherever you fall on this spectrum, you will absolutely develop a more powerful relationship with your dreams when you begin writing them down. Dreams occur in the three-dimensional space of our imagination. This can be a very confusing and chaotic place that rarely makes any logical sense. Writing is linear and has the effect of taking what is floating around in your mind and grounding it in a structure that will allow you to begin working with it in a manageable way. Also, the very words you choose can become as informative and valuable as the dream itself.

After all, the way you remember and describe your dreams also emanates out of your unconscious. How you choose to describe a dream can be interpreted as well, offering additional revealing information about what may be going on inside your head at the time of a dream.

If you don't have time to write down an entire dream, you can choose a few key images and record those. When you come back to them, the images may trigger a deeper sense of the dream, even if you have consciously forgotten it.

Always notice the feelings that come up when writing down your dream. Record whether or not the dream itself had an emotional component. Also notice what emotional state the dream left you in when you woke up, as how a dream leaves you feeling is an important clue in the game of deciphering the hidden information it has to offer you. Additionally, it is important to date your entries so that you can make correlations between dreams and life events as you look back on what you were dreaming about at certain times in your life.

Universality: The Language of Dreams

Dreams are stories told in a language all their own. That language is symbolic in nature. The inherent meaning behind the pictures that appear in dreams is held within the image itself. In order to comprehend this, we must first understand what is meant by "universal."

Something is considered to be universal when it would be easily recognized or understood by most people. The greater the number of people who connect to something, the more universal that thing is. Love is a universal concept because most human beings understand what love feels like. Fear is another one of these familiarly experienced emotions. Most of us can relate to love and fear as universal elements of being alive and human. This concept applies to broad emotional experiences as well as to smaller notions such as forces of nature, people, animals, and objects of all kinds.

The trick to understanding the universal meaning behind any image that appears in a dream is to consider it. What is it? What does it do? What is its use? What is the essence of it? What might most people agree upon when considering that thing? By asking these sorts of questions, any symbol can be interpreted based on this notion that there is a universal language that makes up all dreams.

If you look to chapter 4 on dream archetypes, you will see this concept of universality exemplified many times over. One of the easiest ways to understand this is with the meanings ascribed to animals, the symbolism of which has been handed down over millennia through First Nations of the world. There is no secret to this wisdom; if you look objectively at these descriptions, it becomes very clear that the meaning carried by an animal as a totem is based directly on the energetic quality of the animal itself. Bears have ferocious strength, but they are also an animal that hibernates; in this way, they hold the symbolic meaning of both strength and patience. Deer are graceful creatures that are hyper-alert to their environment in order to stay safe; their symbolic meaning connects to this quality of sensitivity and heightened awareness.

One of the most effective ways to discover the universal meaning for an object is by examining its use or essence. While the use of something applies to its function, its essence connects to its purpose. Although these terms may seem barely distinguishable from each other, they are in fact quite different. Use takes into account what something does, thereby helping define how we relate to it and how it relates to us. On the other hand, the essence of something connects to its purpose, thereby informing us of why we relate to it the way we do.

A refrigerator keeps a certain amount of confined space at a specific desired temperature that is colder than the room in which it stands. This is what it does, which therefore defines its use. Its essence connects to its purpose, which is to lengthen the life of perishable foods. So imagine that a woman describes a dream in which she finds a disembodied head in a refrigerator. Using the principle of universality, the head represents thoughts or ideas that she has not incorporated into her day-to-day thinking. The refrigerator is going to keep the head cold, for certain, but the reason the head is to be kept cold is in order to preserve and extend the life of something we want to keep fresh. In this case, it may be the thoughts that aren't quite attached to the dreamer but can be preserved for later use.

To further illustrate this concept, take the example of a bomb appearing in a dream. Its use relates to creating sudden, intense combustion. It isn't until the essence of deliberate destructiveness toward an implied target is added to the definition that you would have something with which to work. If you had a dream that you were carrying a bomb from one place to another, you could now consider the danger of sudden combustion as well as deliberate destructiveness that the bomb represents. Inherent in this destructive impulse is the desire to eradicate something that exists in order to make way for something new. These minute distinctions will pay huge dividends when the symbols with which you are working are of a more esoteric nature and, therefore, more challenging.

Let's look at a few more examples to make this concept of universality as clear as possible. A hat is used to cover and protect the head. The essence of a hat is to adorn and express yourself. Because a hat is worn on the head, the symbolic meaning must connect with the concept of thoughts or thinking. Therefore, the universal meaning of a hat in a dream will connect to protecting or hiding your private thoughts, but with the added texture of expressing your public thoughts in a creative way.

A jar is often used to hold or contain liquid or fluid substances, whereas its essence relates to the preservation of what's inside it. In a dream, the universal meaning of a jar embodies the need to preserve something or a sense that something from the past is still currently available to you because it has been preserved by your unconscious through the symbol of the jar. The use of a pool is to hold a large amount of water. Its essence aligns with relaxation and fun. Because water is always symbolically associated with emotions, an interpretive meaning that is connected to a pool's use would be a gathering of emotions, whereas a meaning that grounds itself in a pool's essence might connect to a need for more freedom or levity. Both are credible interpretations.

It is very important to note here that there is no one right interpretation and other wrong ones or less effective ways to consider the meaning of a dream image. If a particular symbol holds a very powerful personal association (see the section on free association later in this chapter), that takes precedence over something that has to be figured out in order to make sense. This is an intuitive and irrational process, and whatever feels right should be considered over and above anything that is explored intellectually.

People in Your Dreams

Dreams are filled with people. Some you know, while others are strangers. Sometimes you know exactly who the person is despite the fact that they may look nothing like the person they seem to be representing. And while dreams feature a myriad of settings, objects, themes, and creatures—the list is endless—the bulk of our dreams contain people more than any other type of image.

There is one approach in dream work that asserts that everyone in your dream is a part of you. While this is not the only way to approach the people who appear in your dreams, this is what will be presented here, as it is the closest to the classical Jungian approach. This is not to say that dreams that involve people close to you in your life are not reflecting the relationships you have with them. They are. However, considering every person who appears in a dream as representing a part of your own personality is perhaps the most insightful technique to use when interpreting a dream.

In the same way that it is common for us to express ourselves with language, such as "part of me feels one way and part of me feels another," people tend to organize their inner experience in such a compartmentalized way. This helps us to make sense of the complexity of our mind. Dreams operate according to the same principle, but in a symbolic way: people in your dreams are symbolic representations of different aspects of yourself. One way to work with this principle is to boil it down to something very simple. Choose three adjectives that best describe a person you know from your life who appears in a dream.

As an example, let's say a woman dreams of a teacher she once had who was very analytical and, at times, harshly critical. When this teacher shows up in a dream, the dreamer is connecting to the critical part of herself. Yet another individual dreams of a close friend who is warm and affectionate. As the friend appears in the dreaming landscape, it is these qualities of the dreamer that are best expressed by this person from her waking life.

To break down how this might work in a more direct fashion, let's consider the woman just described who had the dream that her high school English teacher was standing at the back of the conference room in which the dreamer was soon to give a presentation at work. When thinking of three adjectives to describe the English teacher, the dreamer offered "negative," "harsh," and "demanding." When applying the location of the dream (the conference room at work) to her waking life, there was a natural association to how nervous she was about the upcoming presentation. By examining this teacher as an aspect of herself—the negative, harsh, and critical parts—she was able to relieve some of her anxiety by understanding that she is her own worst critic.

The better you know someone from your life, the harder it may be to envision them as operating as a part of your own personality. In these cases, it's best to attempt to stay very detached in your thinking. You might consider how someone else might describe such a person in order to reach a more objective sense of them as an aspect of yourself.

Of course, the dream world is just as populated with people you have never met before, if not more so. When this is the case, use whatever information you have from the dream and any details you can remember about them. The less data offered by the dream, the more work you will have to do to discover what aspect of yourself might be represented by these strangers.

Sometimes this is not at all easy to do, especially if someone in your dream represents elements of your personality that you don't readily relate to. As an example, let's consider a woman in her late twenties who had a dream about an older female boss she worked for many years prior to when she had the dream. The three adjectives she came up with to describe her boss were "aggressive," "powerful," and "unethical." The boss in the dream was representing the part of the dreamer that is also capable of being ruthless and unconcerned with the moral constructs of right and wrong. However, in waking life, this young woman is anything but ruthless. This made it

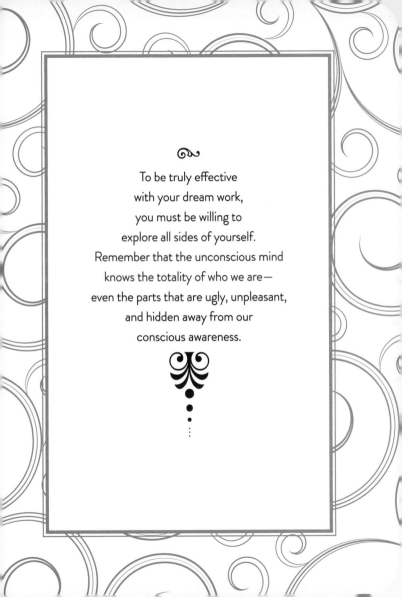

To be truly effective
with your dream work,
you must be willing to
explore all sides of yourself.
Remember that the unconscious mind
knows the totality of who we are—
even the parts that are ugly, unpleasant,
and hidden away from our
conscious awareness.

difficult for her to identify with these qualities in herself, even though as a human being they live within her just as all qualities live within all people.

To be truly effective with your dream work, you must be willing to explore all sides of yourself. Remember that the unconscious mind knows the totality of who we are—even the parts that are ugly, unpleasant, and hidden away from our conscious awareness.

Remembering Your Dreams

If you think that because you don't remember your dreams that means you don't have them, think again. Research has shown that our day-to-day capacity to function properly and the clearing off of the brain through REM sleep and dreaming are intricately bound together. If you didn't dream, then after two or three days you would begin to hallucinate and have great difficulty distinguishing between the data you were receiving from the world moment by moment and other information stored inside your frontal cortex from previous days. So if you are not experiencing a psychotic break right now, you probably had dreams last night.

We don't all have the same capacity to remember our dreams, and for some people it is much easier than for others. There is no known reason why this is the case, other than taking into account differences in individual wiring from person to person. Much like a sense of direction, all human beings are oriented toward the space they are in, but some people possess a clearer sense of where they have moved. There is no meaning to being unable to remember your dreams. There is nothing wrong with people who cannot remember their dreams; it is simply a matter of individual wiring and habit.

Consider that the part of the brain that is awake, alert, and aware of our surroundings is a completely different structure from those areas of the brain that connect in such a way that dreams are the result. In fact, the primary visual cortex, the area of the brain that decodes information coming through the eyes, is tremendously active once we are awake but is not at all connected to the inner visual processing of dream imagery. There are other parts of the frontal cortex that are responsible for cognitive functioning and snap into attention when we wake up; this is so even if your subjective experience of that is not quite so immediate; that is to say, even if you are slow to wake up fully, your waking mind activates immediately as you arouse from sleep.

One way of thinking of this is that the sleeping voice is very soft and the waking voice is very loud. Even if there is some overlap when we wake up, the more active brain functions can completely drown out the dreaming experience. For some people, this switching of gears is so dramatic and habitual that the resulting experience is that they have no memory of the dreams out of which they are emerging when they wake up and start their day. All of this being said, anyone can increase their capacity to remember and retain their dream experiences, though for some the effort required may be greater than for others. There are three essential ingredients to this recipe: intention, preparation, and follow-through.

As with anything you want to create in your life, it is crucial to start to remember your dreams by setting the intention to do so. The unconscious mind responds to the conscious requests we send its way. Of course, the more energy you put behind this idea, the more likely it will be effective. A passing thought of "I hope I remember my dreams tonight" is one thing, but a powerful declaration that "I will remember my dreams tonight" carries more weight. Writing your intention down in a dream journal takes it one step further, for the unconscious mind responds to the physical action of pen to paper as something more solid than a random thought floating around in your mind.

Taking this to an extreme by turning it into a ritual not only is a way to increase the potential efficacy of your desire but can also become a beautiful practice of self-care in and of itself. Distractions are everywhere in our modern world, and allowing yourself to be sucked into their influence before bedtime can have an adverse effect on the depth and restfulness of your sleep and the speed and grace with which you get there. Making the half hour or so before bedtime a sacred act is a powerful ritual and can yield impressive results in the realm of relaxation and the release of stress. Adding the intention of remembering your dreams to such a practice raises the stakes exponentially.

What this might look like is pretty simple. Put your phone away as a start. Turn off the TV as well. Focus on all of the things you generally do in preparation for bed, such as undressing and any grooming that is part of your process, in an intentional manner. Allow your thoughts to be placed on what you are doing as directly connected to the idea of having a beautiful night of sleep that is deep and restful. Instead of letting your mind randomly wander over the day's events or the next day's obligations, concentrate on the task at hand. Create a mantra for yourself during this process, something like "As I undress, I prepare myself for a night of deep and restful sleep. I wake in the morning having remembered my dreams with clarity and ease." Not only can this assist you in connecting to your dream life, but it can have a big impact on your general levels of stress and anxiety as well.

You need the tools to record your dreams at hand, and this brings us to the step of preparation. If you don't have a pad of paper, a journal, or a recording device next to your bed, you will run the risk of waking up more fully in the morning in search of what you need. Having your tools within arm's reach ensures fewer waking-moment distractions, and putting them there before you go to bed deepens the power of the intention you set.

There is some argument that writing with pen and paper the old-fashioned way might be more directly connected to the brain structures that experience and remember dreams. Writing is indeed a more visceral way to record your dreams, but the new world has moved into the digital age. What is more important is that the mechanism you choose be the one that will likely result in your willingness to actually record your dreams. If using your smartphone or a digital recording device is more likely to get you to attend to this morning process, then have at it. If the rustic sensibility of putting pen to paper inspires you, then go with that.

The third and final element in this approach to increasing your dream memory is by far the most important and the one that seems perhaps the most counterintuitive. You must record some content whether you have a dream to describe or not. If you wish to remember your dreams but you wait for a more inspiring and memorable dream to come, you may be waiting a very long time. Recording your nighttime experience is a powerful message to send to your unconscious mind. By doing this, you are signaling it to leave the window between your dreaming mind and your waking mind open a little longer.

On the mornings when nothing seems to be available in your mind from your dream experience, pick up your pad, journal, or recording device anyway. Even if what you have to write or say is something like, "I don't recall anything from my dreaming experience from last night," say that. Then wait a moment or two. Keep your eyes closed and relax and lean into the still silence of the sleep you are just waking from. Let something (if there is anything at all) emerge in your awareness: a color, a shape, a sensation, an image. If nothing comes, you're done for the day. If something should materialize, no matter how small, faint, or seemingly insignificant, record it. Do this with diligence, and you are likely to see results within a few weeks.

• EXERCISE 1 •

Remembering Your Dreams

STEP ONE: Set the intention to remember your dreams. Do this both as a mental exercise and with regard to how you prepare yourself for sleep.

STEP TWO: Put paper and pen or a recording device by your bedside so you will be ready to record your dreams when you wake.

STEP THREE: In the morning, immediately pick up your paper and pen or recording device before you do anything else, even before you get out of bed.

STEP FOUR: Write or record something, even if you don't have a specific dream to describe.

Doing the Dream Work

Now that you have learned some of the basics about how dreams work, it's time to look at how to work with them.

What follows are several tried-and-true techniques and exercises that will deepen your relationship with your dreams once you have them. Some of them may speak to you more powerfully than others, and you may be drawn toward one or more of them for stretches of time. As I have said a number of times already, there is no right or wrong way to work with your dreams. However, there are certainly approaches that have yielded great results for people over the past century or so. The next sections will give you a smattering of some of the most effective ways to take your dream work to the next level.

Identifying the Theme of a Dream

Part of interpreting a dream can involve the themes that a dream might be expressing about your life at any given moment in time. The risk of introducing this idea is that people might overcomplicate this and therefore miss the value. Thematic consideration is a subtlety of dream work and not a mainstay. As such, it should be treated as something that can add color to your palette, but it should not be confused with the paper and paintbrush you are working with.

Using a movie such as *The Wizard of Oz* might be a good way to make this point clearer. You could identify the meaning of this movie by interpreting the plot: A young girl gets swept into a faraway land where fantastical creatures help her find her way home. You could do the same for the characters themselves: There's a man made entirely of straw and burlap. Another is made of tin. And these are just two characters—there are dozens more and they are equally fascinating.

The symbolic meaning of the strange creatures that populate the land that is located just over the rainbow is rich and varied. But the theme of the film connects with the idea that is the intended message behind all of the plot lines and the characters and how they interact with each other. Here, it has to do with going on a long expedition, only to find one's way back home and the sense of self that can come only after venturing into the depths of the unknown. It is the classic hero's journey. The theme, then, might be expressed like this: You are already home.

Let's look at a dream to illustrate this process. A young man in his late twenties describes a dream in which he was walking his sister's dog. The dream dog was a big, powerful animal that was pulling aggressively on the leash. The dog finally yanked so hard that he jerked the leash out of the dreamer's hand and ran away. In the next scene, the dreamer went to tell his sister what happened—that he lost her dog because he wasn't strong enough to hold him. Her reaction was surprisingly nonchalant.

When working on this dream using a thematic approach, the dreamer is asked to come up with a title of the dream as if it were a movie he had seen. The title he chooses is *Dog Gone Mad*. He chooses this title because of the humorous play on words from a familiar phrase. Now that the dream has a title, it is time to identify the theme. Since in the dream the dreamer was struggling to be in control of something (the dog), the theme he assigns to the dream is of being effective in the world. So we have a title and a theme and are now free to consider what the dream is trying to tell him.

Going back to the title, he notices that he chose to include the word *mad* in it. Combining the theme and the title, we are clearly involved in an investigation of the dreamer's effectiveness (or lack thereof) in the world and just how mad he is about that. Now the doors really open up: he wonders why his sister didn't show any anger in the dream when he was certain, based on her personality, that she would. She is, in fact, nonchalant and accepting in the dream, whereas in waking life she would be anything but.

In this family, the dreamer was never shown how to express feelings of anger directly. Instead, he learned how to battle for control in less obvious and passive-aggressive ways. In his own life, by acting nonchalant toward his own anger, it shows up as conflict that seems to come out of nowhere and where there is no winner. He would not have made these connections without the introduction of the title and the theme he chose to work with. In this way, approaching the dream work from a thematic perspective, the level of the interpretation was deeper and of more value.

• EXERCISE 2 •
Identifying the Theme of a Dream

STEP ONE: Write your dream down.

STEP TWO: Think of a title for your dream and write that down.

STEP THREE: After ruminating on what the dream means to you, consider what the theme of the dream might be and write that in your journal.

Rumination

To ruminate on something is to contemplate it over and over again. This is the simplest form of dream work, and you have most likely already practiced this without even knowing it. If you've ever simply thought about a dream you had, you've practiced the art of rumination. The thing that transforms it from daydreaming into an actual tool is the magic ingredient of intention. Thinking about something over and over again is at best a distraction and at worst an obsession, neither of which is helpful for the person doing the thinking. But adding intention to the process changes everything.

If you look up the word *intention* in the dictionary, it basically has something to do with purpose. In the world of self-investigation, however, it has a much more powerful meaning. In this regard, an intention is an emotionally charged idea that is the magic ingredient you add to any activity; it has the power to raise the stakes of the experience you desire to have. You can purge your closets and the result will be more room for storage. Add the intention of clearing out the psychic debris of things you haven't paid attention to in a while, and you will experience a significant shift in your level of serenity.

Adding intention to ruminating about a dream allows the mind to propel this spontaneous process into a powerful level of self-investigation. The intention is to focus gently on the dream as you review it over and over so that, in an organic way, new ideas, fresh perspectives, and spontaneous associations can occur to you, rising up out of your unconscious mind. Ultimately, the intention for all dream work is to have a deeper experience of yourself and the level of consciousness through which you respond to all that happens in your life.

This process is most effective if you have written your dream down. Set yourself up in a quiet place where you are not likely to be disturbed. Take what you have written and read it back to yourself. Then read it again. When you have read through it twice, do so at least one more time. Your mind will probably interrupt this process with random thoughts. When this occurs, gently bring your attention back to the dream. However, also do your best to be mindful about where your thoughts drift. As you begin reliving the dream in your mind's eye, some of these random thoughts may in fact connect to the dream. Slowly, associations, interpretations, or related ideas may gently enter your conscious mind and expand your understanding of the meaning of the dream.

If you have an active mind with a lot of chatter that is not easily quieted, you may think this technique is not for you. On the contrary, with patience for the inevitable dead ends and alleys that are often the byproducts of a busy head, this process can be surprisingly effective and has the added benefit of being a meditative discipline. Rumination is also something that can be done with another person or group in the form of discussion. In fact, every time you describe a dream to an acquaintance, friend, or loved one, you are actually engaging in this form of dream work. Having people in your life with whom you can discuss your dreams fosters intimacy and offers a powerful sounding board for creating a satisfying experience of considering a dream.

Here is a dream in which rumination was the primary modality of the interpretation. A man in his thirties had this dream while he was exploring a relationship with a woman he had recently met.

I dreamed I was driving my SUV at a high rate of speed, and the woman I'm currently dating was in the passenger seat. Suddenly, the car veered slightly. After regaining control, I apologized for driving too fast. A police car appeared in front of me. I decided to follow what became a caravan of police cars setting a slow and deliberate speed, which made me feel safe. Then we hit a patch of ice, which caused me to lose control and the truck went over a cliff. I knew we were going to die. I was comfortable with my own death but had a wave of guilt about killing the girl and about the reaction of her family.

While ruminating on this dream, the truck was the first image that stuck out for the dreamer, as it was the actual truck he drives every day. This lets us know that we are investigating how his life is currently moving and where it is (or isn't) going. When making associations about the woman in the passenger seat, he confirmed that he was indeed dating her in his waking life and that he was feeling ambivalent about continuing the relationship. After going deeper, he revealed that not only was he not sure he wanted to continue the relationship, but he was having a lot of feelings come up around what it would be like to end the relationship and experience the fallout from other people's reactions to that choice.

The next element of the dream that stood out for the dreamer was the moment when he apologized for driving too fast. Ruminating about this idea revealed his own tendency to drive aggressively and that it seemed odd that he felt the need to apologize in the dream for driving fast. Before long, he was wondering whether he was really talking (in his dream) about the movement toward commitment—it was the relationship that was moving too fast.

When thinking about the patch of ice, he began to express what ice actually is: frozen water. His very next thought was, "I guess my feelings for her are starting to cool off." So not only did his icy feelings impact how he was moving down the road of his life, but they had the additional impact of sending him over a cliff, clearly indicating the demise of the connection between him and his significant other.

With all that had been revealed thus far, the dreamer was now recognizing that the most important reaction to the accident in the dream was his concern over how his passenger had been affected. Indeed, he was more preoccupied with how her family and friends would view his culpability in the crash than with the event itself. As a result of interpreting this dream, the dreamer was able to confront his struggles around being concerned about what other people think and how this preoccupation had been keeping him from doing what was right and best for him, even if that meant hurting someone he cared about.

· EXERCISE 3 ·
Rumination

STEP ONE: Write down your dream in as much detail as you can remember.

STEP TWO: Sit in a quiet place and relax to get centered.

STEP THREE: Read your dream out loud. Repeat this several times.

STEP FOUR: Go back through the dream step by step and either speak out loud or write down your thoughts, observations, or new ideas that emerge spontaneously.

Free Association

The role that free association plays in psychoanalysis and dream work is nothing short of remarkable. In the early treatment of mental illness, big strides were made using the newly discovered technique of hypnosis. With hypnosis, physicians found it possible to learn things about their

When free association is
used as a constructive tool,
especially when the images
that appear in dreams are
the subject matter,
truly remarkable information
can be culled from the
depths of the psyche.

patients' fantasies and hidden thoughts that turned out to be quite profound and revelatory.

The unconscious mind is always engaged with us and eagerly waits for moments to express itself. It does this in the words we choose to use and in the details of a story we might leave out and other details we might add, even if they aren't quite true. The association from one thought to another is so revealing that if people were truly aware of how much they expose in this way, most would go about life never uttering a word. However, when free association is used as a constructive tool, especially when the images that appear in dreams are the subject matter, truly remarkable information can be culled from the depths of the psyche.

Free association is probably most effectively used in modern psychotherapy when it comes to dream work. It's a simple process that involves taking a symbol that appears in a dream and making an association with another image based on the original. Though this works well in the consulting room, it can be done on your own and might be made easier as a writing process. It plays out as a function of asking yourself, "What does that make you think of?"

This way of working with dreams allows for a free-flowing expression of the unconscious and may take the dreamer to some surprising places. It does not require working with the meaning that a symbol might have in a universal fashion, but rather the specific and personal trigger that the image creates for the dreamer.

A dream dictionary might depict dreaming of flying a kite in a park as soaring to new heights on an intellectual level while at the same time staying grounded in what is familiar. And yet, the dreamer, who has a childhood memory of feeling humiliated while flying a kite at a park, finds that the dream sparks the need to explore moments of childhood feelings of inadequacy, even though the dream itself was filled with pleasant imagery and sensations. The dreamer wrote the following in his journal:

> When I was a kid, we did a lot of kite flying in the park. I was woefully inadequate at getting the thing off the ground, and as a result, I did not enjoy this experience. Not ever. Suddenly, thinking about that, I remember that feeling of complete inadequacy and how much the rest of my family just left me in the dust, like I didn't matter. Then I would cry and my brother would make fun of me for that.

Now the dreamer has a deeper expression of his unconscious to explore. There may be some current-life experience that is reminding him of inadequacy and abandonment. The point is that a powerful association does not have to be rational; in fact, the more illogical the association you make, the more likely you are tapping into something unconscious. This process requires an absence of judgment or second-guessing and should be done quickly and impulsively. In other words, trust your intuition and don't think too much. This is, in reality, a visceral experience and not a mental one.

Free association is a simple way of uncovering surprising depth and meaning in your dream work and can be used any time you feel stuck while trying to pinpoint an elusive interpretation. Pick an image from a dream, perhaps one that stands out in your mind. Then take the symbol in question and make an association and see where it leads you. You can do this with a partner who listens or as part of a discussion, or you can do it in written form on your own as a part of journaling.

For example, a man had a dream with a puppy in it. When asked to make an association for "puppy," he told a story about when he was a boy and had kept a puppy under the porch for three days before his mother found out and made him give it away. Since dogs represent loyalty and enthusiastic affection, the dream clearly involved these qualities in the dreamer's life. By adding the association of the sad moment when he had to give up the love and affection the puppy provided, he was able to dramatically access more potent material with which to work. In this way, he could apply what he discovered to the circumstances in his current life.

Here is another example. A woman dreamed of a large warehouse where she was held prisoner by an unseen authority. A warehouse is a storage facility. This setting tells us she's examining old material that she's been storing up for many years. When asked to free-associate about this image, she ruminated that warehouses store things, like clothes. From there, she made associations about what clothes mean to her. This led to a story about getting ready for her high school prom, which in turn led her to an association with not being thin enough for her liking.

The dream dislodged a previously denied body-image issue that had been troubling her on an unconscious level all her life. This dream and the associations that followed allowed the woman, now in her early thirties, to see that the unknown authority that held her prisoner was her own self-judgment about her body and her eating habits. Remember that a warehouse can store an almost inexhaustible array of different things, but her particular association was to clothes. Her unconscious was working with her to bring these specific body-image issues into her conscious awareness so she could address them with more clarity.

When the image of the prom popped into her head seemingly out of nowhere, it surprised her. Free association is an organic process, and your mind will indeed surprise and sometimes delight you. You cannot make a wrong association. Do your best to allow ideas to flow spontaneously, without holding back or judging what comes up for you. If an association doesn't feel like it has hit something important, make an association to the image that does come, and your unconscious will deliver more hints to your mind.

One technique for doing this on your own is to write your associations in list form, stopping when you land on something that feels important. Using the previous sample dream, our dreamer might have written a list like this:

> *Warehouse*
>
> *Storage*
>
> *Clothes*

Fashion

Popularity

<u>*Prom Night*</u>

This last association is underlined because it was the one that sparked an epiphany in the dreamer. This is how you know you've landed somewhere of value and made a powerful free association for yourself—when you widen your eyes and say to yourself, "Now that's interesting!"

Here's another example of how to use free association. In this case, a dream about an unknown house connected the dreamer to a house from his childhood that contained some very potent memories. The man dreamed of being in a lavish house. The dream consisted primarily of him wandering through the house, going from room to room, looking for some unknown but important thing, which he never was able to find. He woke up feeling frustrated and angry.

When the man practiced free association regarding the house in the dream, the first thought that emerged was the similarity of the dream house to the beautiful home of a childhood friend. Associating further, he thought about a particular evening when he had stayed over for dinner at that house. He remembered an embarrassing incident where he ate a great deal of food at the dinner table only to get sick and have to excuse himself to go to the bathroom periodically to throw up. This led to him associating the house with utter humiliation and feeling terribly embarrassed. Here is his list of associations:

> *House*
>
> *Wealth*
>
> *Vomiting*
>
> *Embarrassment*
>
> *Rejection*
>
> *Undeserving*

The interpretation starts with the dreamer searching for his sense of self (houses represent the self in dreams) and being unable to do so, as represented by the unfound object. The process of free association adds the element of emotional embarrassment and feeling undeserving of abundance, as represented by the richness of the surroundings in the dream house. Ironically, this man was about to start a new, very high-paying job, and this dream was allowing him to process his strong undercurrent of feeling undeserving when it came to accepting abundance in his life.

• EXERCISE 4 •
Free Association

STEP ONE: Write down your dream in as much detail as you can remember.

STEP TWO: Sit in a quiet place and relax to get centered.

STEP THREE: Pick a single image from your dream narrative.

STEP FOUR: Write down or speak what that image inspires you to think about.

STEP FIVE: Continue this process, from inspired image to inspired image, until you feel a sense of satisfaction and completion.

Automatic Handwriting

Automatic handwriting is a technique that Jung developed while he was in what he usually referred to as his "creative illness," or what is more commonly known as the "dark night of the soul." During such times of existential crisis, the threshold between the conscious and the unconscious is the most easily traversed. Jung understood this and took advantage of this availability to explore areas of the psyche that generally remain hidden.

One of the tools that Jung stumbled upon during this time was automatic handwriting. He had already formulated the theory that the various characters he encountered in his dream world lived inside his unconscious mind. When he would awaken from powerful dreams, he would do anything he could to keep the connection to his unconscious open and available. In an attempt to do this, he decided to communicate with one of the characters directly through journaling.

Jung recognized that his dominant hand, the one with which he did all his writing, was intrinsically bound to his conscious mind. Might then his non-dominant hand offer some indirect connection to his unconscious? The experiment worked. He indeed found that if he sat down with a particular dream character in mind and wrote out a question on the page with his dominant hand and then switched the pen to his other hand, a fascinating thing occurred: thoughts began to pour onto the page that did not appear to be emanating from his ego mind but rather from someplace deeper. The answers always surprised him, and this technique became a staple for Jungian analysts that followed in his footsteps.

Here is an example from a therapy client who was dealing with debilitating chronic pain due to some fused vertebrae in her neck. For a period of several weeks prior to a scheduled surgery, her dreams contained many images of her neck in various expressions of challenge. One featured a beautiful scarf that began to slowly strangle her. In an even more gruesome dream, her head actually began to separate from her body at her neck, with a sort of hinge-like mechanism. These interpretations were so literal because of the specific injury and pending surgery.

In an effort to go a bit deeper, the dreamer used automatic handwriting to see if anything interesting might emerge. Here is what came up when she used the neck pain itself as if it were a character from her dreams.

DREAMER: Okay, neck of mine! You and I seem to be working at cross purposes lately. You have been a real pain in the neck.

NECK PAIN: You are one to talk. It is because of you that I am being this pain. You gotta learn how to speak up!

DREAMER: What was the purpose of your coming on as such a strong pain when I first saw Dr. Jones?

NECK PAIN: Because you were following Dorothy down the yellow brick road, hoping that the healer you were seeking would show you where your home was. The pain was there to teach you to listen to your own knowing. And just like Dorothy, you found the old man behind the curtain. You had all the answers the whole time.

DREAMER: So you mean I didn't actually believe I was going to get better?

NECK PAIN: You felt that your healing was not up to you. Your pain got worse because you were giving too much power to others—the doctors, the "experts." Sometimes they're wrong!

DREAMER: Geez, you are very preachy. You seem like you think you know it all. I decided to go to Dr. Jones. I thought I was following my own guidance.

NECK PAIN: Uh huh … so what did you find?

DREAMER: I did strengthen my connection to myself and to the Divine, but not because of … (pause). I don't understand why you are being so tenacious about being a pain in my neck.

NECK PAIN: This is reality, baby. You have a lot of years of wear and tear. Accidents and aging have made me a little rusty and frozen from lack of use. I need some outside intervention. Dr. Jones may be just great, but you are the one who has to believe it's possible and be willing to say so out loud.

This woman didn't realize just how much her thoughts and the challenges she was having with her spiritual belief system were impacting how much pain she was in. This automatic handwriting completely changed how she interacted with her surgeon and other physicians. She is well on her way now to living a much more pain-free existence.

Another dreamer, a woman in her forties, was preparing to go to nursing school in order to expand her career opportunities in the health field in which she works. As she was about to take a math test that is part of qualifying for the advanced-level course of study, she had this dream:

I dreamed I was at the airport preparing to travel to Mexico and realized I had forgotten my purse. In a panic, I went to call my ex-husband to ask him to

> bring it to me, but I couldn't remember the phone
> number and I couldn't find it in the phone book.

This dreamer was indeed feeling ill-prepared for what lay ahead of her. Phone numbers represent access to effective communication with others, especially in times of need. Forgetting the phone number may have reflected her sense of isolation and an inability to connect to her support system. Interestingly, in this case it was her ex-husband she was looking to for help. He was definitely not a current member of her inner circle at the time of the dream.

Not remembering the digits necessary to reach him offered an additional ironic and subtle interpretation: In her waking life, she was experiencing fears about her knowledge and skills. Comfort with numbers would be essential for her performance on the pending math examination she would soon face. Additionally, she was traveling to a country where they speak Spanish, something akin to taking a test where the language of math is more foreign than familiar.

All of these interpretations were accurate and insightful, and they resonated with the dreamer on a cerebral level. However, she continued to feel dissatisfied; it was far too troubling a dream to be dismissed as just

• • • • • • • • • • • • • • • • • •

Jung found that if
he sat down with a particular
dream character in mind and
wrote out a question on the page
with his dominant hand
and then switched the pen
to his other hand,
a fascinating thing occurred:
thoughts began to pour onto the page
that did not appear to be emanating
from his ego mind
but rather from someplace deeper.

an expression of stress about math class. In order to go deeper, she did some automatic handwriting with the other character that appeared in the dream, her ex-husband. Here is what came up:

DREAMER: I've been trying to reach you. I need my purse.

EX-HUSBAND: What's that got to do with me?

DREAMER: I need you to bring it to me.

EX-HUSBAND: You can't do anything right. Do I have to do everything for you?

DREAMER: What's that supposed to mean?

EX-HUSBAND: This is why I always had to do everything.

DREAMER: Well, not anymore. That's why I left you.

EX-HUSBAND: You are lost without me.

DREAMER: You are so wrong about that. You don't have any control over me anymore!

This automatic handwriting brought up a lot of emotions for the dreamer, and it helped her reach a deep and full understanding of the dream. She recognized that she was anxious about going back to school and passing the math test; it was, in fact, a bit of a hurdle for her to get over. But the deeper meaning revealed by the automatic handwriting connected to the ways in which her ex-husband had always held her back. In leaving him, she took the risk of freeing herself from his controlling ways, but the dream illuminated that she was still stuck in this same pattern of not fully taking control of her own life and destiny.

• EXERCISE 5 •
Automatic Handwriting

STEP ONE: Pick a dream that you would like to work with.

STEP TWO: Create a sacred space where you will be free from distractions.

STEP THREE: Identify a character in your dream that you feel moved to dialogue with.

STEP FOUR: Formulate a question that you would like to ask this character, and write it down with your dominant hand.

STEP FIVE: Switch the pen to your non-dominant hand and just begin writing your response to the question without thinking.

STEP SIX: If working with your non-dominant hand feels too challenging when recording your response, simply use a different writing implement, such as a different-colored pen.

Petitioning Dreams

One of the most interesting and powerful aspects of dream work takes the form of actually asking your dreams to offer you specific guidance on matters of importance in your life. This is known as petitioning your dreams and is really quite simple. You ask a question and treat the dream that follows as your answer. While this can be done casually, as a simple thought before bedtime, the more intention you put into the process, the more likely you will be to receive a powerful response. You might even write the request down in the form of a letter to your higher self or as an entry in a dream journal.

For example, a woman in her early thirties had been dating a man for three months. In many ways he was quite enjoyable, but there were ways that his unavailability was beginning to trouble her. There seemed to be themes showing up that reminded her of previous relationships in which she was ready for more commitment than the men she was involved with, and she was no longer willing to ignore the red flags that seemed to be revealing themselves. She had done enough personal work to recognize the lifelong patterns that the dating world helped illuminate. In the past, she had invested quite a bit in men who did not show up for her, and this was the first time she was preparing to end something much sooner. However, just to be sure, she petitioned her dreams, asking for guidance on what to do about this particular man. This is the dream that came:

> I was at a celebration that I knew was an anniversary of a relationship, like a wedding anniversary. After a bit, I realized that I was one of the people in this couple and I secretly knew that I no longer wanted to be married. But no one at the party knew this and not my husband either. He was off in the other room and I was aware that he had been behaving badly earlier in the night, which is why he had left the room. Then he came into the room as the party was breaking up and it was my father. Not someone like my father, MY ACTUAL FATHER. I couldn't believe it. When I woke up,

I was actually laughing. I had married my father. How crazy is that!?

This is a perfect example of the power of dream petitioning. By recognizing that once again she was indeed playing out the challenges of a father who was unable to be expressive and loving, she had attracted a potential mate who was exhibiting the same behaviors. By making such a direct connection between her dream life and her waking life, she was able to comfortably end the relationship without any of the self-doubt that had inhibited her in the past.

Not all dreams will be this direct. Part of the process is to trust whatever dream comes, even if you don't even remember one in the morning. The unconscious mind is a powerful and mysterious force. Just by asking the question, it is answered, even if that happens behind the scenes and beneath your awareness. The same is true for a dream that you do remember but that feels unclear as to how it relates to your question. Part of trusting this process is living more in the question and the mystery and less in the answer and the false clarity of intellectual understanding.

• EXERCISE 6 •
Petitioning Your Dreams

STEP ONE: Prepare for bedtime with a sense of it being a sacred act.

STEP TWO: Take a moment to be quiet and reflective before turning in.

STEP THREE: Write a petition or ask aloud for your dreams to provide an answer or guidance with regard to a specific issue that you are currently facing in your life.

STEP FOUR: In the morning, write down whatever dreams come. Even if no dream is remembered, trust that you have received the guidance you have asked for.

Dream Circles

A dream circle is a gathering of people who share their dreaming experiences at the community level. These can range from formal, regularly scheduled meetings led by a trained facilitator to informal social events where dreams are casually shared by those who join. Motivated enthusiasts are generally behind the formation of such groups, and there really is no structure created by any authority as to how to approach the process. In other words, there are no rules for creating a dream circle.

There are, however, some pitfalls to be avoided. The primary one is a phenomenon known as projection, whereby a person responding to someone else's dream does not realize how much they are actually speaking about themselves. As an example, a dreamer shares a dream involving their spouse that includes some relationship conflict. A member of the circle comments about the dream, certain that it means that the marriage in question is in terrible danger and perhaps a breakup is imminent. However, the dreamer is in a happy, committed relationship and the commenter is not. The listener is adding content and meaning to the dream that may not actually be there because they are listening through the lens of their own experience. This can set up a challenging dynamic between dream circle members, and if there is no facilitator to navigate this issue, projection can dismantle the harmony that is necessary for any group to sustain itself.

There is a protocol for discussing dreams that can help members circumnavigate this challenge. It asks people to use the language "If this were my dream, ..." before adding any personal perspective that the dream they have heard is triggering for them. This accomplishes several important things. First, it puts the speaker in a position of ownership of their words, ensuring that what they are saying is coming from them and is not a projection onto the dreamer. It implies an agreement that no matter what is said, whoever is speaking is referring only to themselves and not attempting to guide, advise, or offer an opinion about the dreamer or the dream being discussed.

To elaborate using the previous example, the commenter can now say, "If this were my dream, the conflict in the bedroom might represent a desire to end the relationship." Problem solved. Each person is respected and emotional boundaries are not crossed.

Another way of creating structure to support a positive and unified experience in a dream circle is to approach each dream from the same perspective using a series of questions:

ONE: What is the name of this dream?

TWO: What is the theme of this dream?

THREE: How did this dream make you feel?

FOUR: What do you think this dream is telling you?

Dreams are stories, and when you weave together the dreams of more than one person gathering at the community level, a new story emerges, one that is often driven by the mysterious way that life has of drawing the right people together at just the right time. One way of tapping into this mysterious experience is to allow the order in which the dreams are shared to be left to the power of synchronicity.

Have every person in the dream circle put their name in a hat. The leader, or one chosen individual, picks the first dreamer to share. When that dreamer is done, that person picks the next individual to go. This allows the power of the collective unconscious to have a voice in how the group's message is expressed. Very often, the themes that emerge and the seemingly coincidental connections that become apparent when a group is approached in this manner are filled with delight and rich with inspiration.

• EXERCISE 7 •

Creating a Dream Circle

STEP ONE: Contact your friends and associates to find interested people.

STEP TWO: Pick a space and time that works for most people's schedules.

STEP THREE: Establish a leader or facilitator, if that feels important.

STEP FOUR: Create structure and boundaries in advance and stick to them.

Creative Expression and Dream Work

Dreams are messages from the unconscious mind and are written in a language that is symbolic in nature. The linear, rational mind is what we use to consider what our dreams may mean to us, but these two domains of processing information (the conscious mind and the unconscious mind) are so different that they are almost incompatible. If the unconscious mind is attempting to communicate with the conscious mind through symbolic expression, the best way to let the unconscious know that you have heard the call is to respond in the same manner.

This back-and-forth narrative is something that occurs between the dreaming life and the waking life of the dreamer all on its own. However, when you work with a dream in any fashion, the stakes are raised in that narrative, which any person who has worked with their dreams will attest to. And while any element of dream work can yield satisfying results, it is arguable that removing the rational, thinking mind completely is crucial to having a more profound experience of considering a dream. In this way, using creative expression as a form of dream work is possibly the most satisfying approach through which to encourage a dynamic relationship between a person and their unconscious mind.

One of the things that is necessary for this approach to work well is to fully remove any sense of artistic excellence being a necessary ingredient to make the process either successful or satisfying. The unconscious mind is not an art critic. Sitting down and putting some creative focus on a dream or a dream image does not require any skill or talent. It will be best if you can allow yourself to be free of the inhibitions that sometimes come with judging your creative impulses.

Any creative act can be used for this purpose, including drawing, writing, poetry, movement, sculpture, or collage. If you can think it up, you can use it to your advantage. The most important element of this approach is to treat the experience as a sacred act. Make sure you won't be interrupted. Gather everything you think you might need. Perhaps you would like to light a candle or play some soothing music. Then recall a dream, an image from a dream, or a character that appeared in a dream that you want to work with, and have at it. There are no rules and there is no end result to chase. It is through the creative act itself that the unconscious mind is stimulated.

In this approach to dream work, what you are cultivating is an ongoing conversation between your unconscious mind (in the form of dreams) and your conscious mind (in its response to them through dream work). Over time, you will definitely develop a sense of the influence that expanding this dialogue will have over your sense of self-investigation. When that happens, you will also know intuitively when a dream or dream image wants to be honored in this way.

It is a growing trend for formal dream work (such as the kind that takes place in workshop settings) to take this idea to truly advanced levels. Using dream imagery to generate movement and artistic expression of all kinds at a group level can be both healing and insightful. There are even acting teachers working with very successful actors in Hollywood who specialize in using dreams and dream interpretation as part of their approach to roles and character development. Accessing the unconscious mind is such a potent aspect of the creative process that incorporating dream work into that can yield amazing results. This is true for the artist and the ordinary person alike.

• EXERCISE 8 •
Creative Expression and Dream Work

STEP ONE: Write down your dream so you have all the details clear in your memory.

STEP TWO: Sit with your dream and allow one particular character or image to inspire your creativity.

STEP THREE: One approach is to draw the image from your dream using whatever materials you have at your disposal. Your skill level is not important, and the drawing does not have to be a literal representation of what you dreamed. Simply intend to express the feelings that are evoked by the dream and the image you are choosing to work with.

STEP FOUR: Once you have a drawing, you can do anything you like with it that feels right—anything from putting it on display to burning it in a sacred ritual.

If there is anything that bears repeating about how to be in a satisfying relationship with your dreams, it is that there is absolutely no one right way to work with them. Conversely, you cannot harm your psyche by attempting to interpret your dreams, no matter what approach you take. Just by recognizing that your dreams have value elevates this organic process to a higher-stakes experience.

By having different options for working with your dreams, as outlined in this chapter, you can pick and choose the approach(es) that speaks to you the most. You can concentrate on a single technique for a time and then switch to other tools that I have described. There are still other methods of dream work that you may stumble upon in your quest for self-exploration. Deepening your interaction with your own dreams will absolutely lead you to a better understanding of yourself as you progress through life.

Chapter Four

DREAM ARCHETYPES

When it comes to dreams, most people have an insatiable desire to understand what they mean. The beauty of the process of working with any dream is that the meaning belongs to the dreamer alone. In this way, there is no such thing as a wrong or bad interpretation.

I once got a phone call from a friend who had a dream about a skunk. We were going to see each other later that day, so I waited until then to hear about the dream. During the time between our call and our meeting several hours later, she used an online dream dictionary to explore the meaning of her dream. The dictionary told her that skunks relate to issues of sexuality. Now, never in a million years would I give a sexual connotation to the skunk. In fact, skunks in my view connect much more to fear and to the powerful smell of their musk that is released when they feel trapped and frightened.

But when I sat with my friend, I could not dismiss the idea that this dream must connect to issues of sexuality, because her process and investigation had led her to that meaning. By putting together thoughts about sexuality and the lingering bad smell that follows a skunk around, we were able to create an interpretation about shame and sexuality that was truly powerful and profound for my friend. This would never have occurred without her veering off into something that I never would have thought to add to the mix.

So a symbol that appears in a dream can mean many things. However, as I outlined in the previous chapter, all images and objects carry within them a universal meaning based on the qualities they possess. This chapter focuses on the most frequently appearing dream structures and archetypes, and the universal meanings associated with each.

Animals

So much of the content of our dreams comes directly from our environment. And while we in our modern world are far more urban than rural, the collective unconscious—the realm of unconscious thought that runs through every being on Earth—still retains the powerfully symbolic meaning of animals as clearly now as it did when our First Nations predecessors first began to think about their dreams in a significant way.

Animals in dreams are very powerful symbols. They represent the instinctive nature of human beings, and since they are universal to the entire planet, their meaning is very pure. Animals in the dream world are direct symbols of personal power. The aspects of personal power that they represent are based on the qualities of the animal itself. Even when the animal appearing in a dream seems scary and off-putting, it should be interpreted as a very positive sign. Stepping into one's own personal power is, in fact, a scary proposition.

Consider the essence and energetic qualities of the animal that appears to you. Then recognize that your unconscious mind is letting you know that not only do you need this quality in order to face some element of your life right

❧

Animals in dreams are very
powerful symbols. They represent
the instinctive nature of
human beings,
and since they are universal
to the entire planet,
their meaning
is very pure.

now, but you also have access to this quality. It is pre-installed. Animal dreams were considered a blessing in past civilizations and should be considered this way in our modern world as well.

Here are some of the most common animals that appear in our dreams and their symbolic meanings.

Bear

You need to be patient and conserve your strength for now; the time to act will come after a period of hibernation. Bear medicine is about the long stillness that is necessary in order for true strength to be wielded appropriately. When the time to act comes, the power of the bear in you will give you incredible resources. A dream with a bear in it is asking you to consider whether it is time for aggression or time to retreat and wait for the right season.

Cat

You are dreaming about unconditional love in the feminine principle. Cats of all types represent powerful feminine energy, which includes receptivity, creativity, sensuality, and stillness. They are hunters by nature, and their nocturnal behavior associates them with the feminine aspect of night. While their masculine counterpart, the dog, embodies a pack mentality, the cat is the symbol of self-reliance. First domesticated about three thousand years ago, cats were revered for their ability to control rodent populations that would have beleaguered the stores of grain that were so crucial to the emergence of civilization. Cats have long been associated with magic and witchcraft, with the classic black cat as the carrier of the most superstition.

Crow

All birds are to be considered as messengers of some kind. There is probably no bird that exemplifies this more than the crow or raven. In Norse mythology, the two ravens Huginn and Muninn represent thought and memory; they fly around and report back to Odin every day and create our ability to name things and commit them to memory. They gather where humans do, and so they reflect our numbers directly in proportion to our population. In this way, crows and ravens bring us important messages when they appear in dreams. A group of crows in community is known as a murder, and this twist on words adds an element of shadow to their medicine.

Deer

Grace and beauty are the medicine of this timid animal. Also, the need to be on guard and self-protective is part of what is being called into consciousness when a deer appears in a dream. The deer knows its way through the woods and has the ability to guide us through unknown and hidden territory. If the deer has antlers, this increases its power to navigate through primal instincts.

Dog

You are connecting to principles around unconditional love as expressed by the masculine principle. Dogs represent unbridled joy, constant affection, and enthusiastic loyalty. A dog in your dream connects to your own capacity to remain constant in love and affection. Remember to consider what the dog in your dream is doing and add that to this idea of unconditional love and you will understand what this dream means. The presence of a dog means a need to call this quality into your life, and this image being present in the dream indicates that the quality is readily available. Anything that inhibits this, such as a dog being injured, sick, lost, or challenged in any way, is pointing out your own inhibitions around being loving for love's sake. A dog in your dream connects to loyalty and love, which can indicate that issues of commitment and intimacy are being triggered by some event or circumstance. A positive dream experience could be pointing to places in your life that are sparking enthusiasm or requiring you to become more enthusiastic and joyful. Frightening images involving dogs may be inviting you to investigate unconscious fears around love and connection. A rabid dog represents inner fears of danger that may befall you if you get too close to an intimate situation. An actual dog bite represents the misuse of kindness or consideration. An obedient dog may point to a sense of control in areas of friendship and trust. Different types of dogs can embody a variety of qualities, from the dog that rescues a person in danger to the harrowing attacker. Dogs range in shape, from something tiny enough to put in your pocket to large breeds that resemble small bears. The size and attributes of the dog in your dream will inform you of the scope of the unconscious notions being expressed.

Dove

The dove is a symbol of peace and love, and if one appears in a dream, you are connecting to these principles through the symbolism of the dove itself as well as through the animal medicine that the dove brings. Doves are also symbolically connected to romantic love.

Eagle

All birds are to be considered as messengers of some kind. The eagle, however, is perhaps the most majestic of these air creatures and their medicine is very powerful. It is one of the largest birds and its size and power have led many aboriginal cultures to consider it an earthly incarnation of a godlike presence. The eagle as a symbol embodies strength, courage, and the ability to soar above any difficulty. The vantage point of such heights is a part of what the eagle brings when it appears in a dream.

Elephant

The elephant's sheer size and strength are at the root of the symbolic meaning associated with it. The Hindu god Ganesh has an elephant head and is thought to bring luck by being the remover of obstacles. He will also bring an obstacle if that is in your highest interest. When the elephant appears in a dream, you are being given the medicine of patience, strength, and the capacity to move through anything. Also to be considered is the notion that elephants "never forget." Your dream of an elephant may be asking you to remember something about your authentic self.

Fish

Fish are like ideas that are floating under the surface of your unconscious mind. Dreaming of fish means you are considering what is lurking just below your awareness, the thoughts and feelings that are close enough to be known to you but that you may have to make an effort to get to the heart of. If the fish are colorful and beautiful, they may be representing more creative aspects of your potential expression. Fish in a tank may be the ideas from your unconscious of which you are actually becoming aware. Containing them in a tank may be considering taking action on them, but could also indicate being stuck in a cycle of limiting your creative expression. A live fish out of water reacts violently. In a dream, this could symbolize the awkwardness surrounding vulnerable expression. Eating fish is to experience satisfaction from the constructive use of your ideas and thoughts.

Hawk

All birds are messengers of some sort, but the power of the hawk is its vantage point. Hawks have great intelligence and exceptional eyesight. Their majestic wingspan can take them to very high ground where they can see quite far. When the hawk visits you in the dream state, you are able to take advantage of this ability to see into the distance across both time and space. Hawks are bringers of messages and help point to new directions with confidence and clarity.

Horse

The horse is the ultimate symbol of power. We even use the horse as a measurement of an engine with the term "horsepower." When harnessed, this mighty beast can take you to extremes of speed and strength. As a totem animal, the horse will visit in a dream when you need to be in touch with this visceral energy to move.

Lion

The king of the jungle is a cat and thus resonates as an embodiment of the feminine principle. Courage, decisiveness, leadership, and strength are all parts of this majestic animal totem. When the lion appears in a dream, you are being blessed with some of the most ferocious power available in the world of animal totems.

Owl

You are tapping into the shadow side of your wisdom. Owls are nocturnal animals with a great ability to see and hunt in the dark. This makes them symbolically connected to the darker, more hidden sides of human nature. They help us to navigate the more unseen elements of our humanity. Owls have long been associated with intuition and mysticism, and in some traditions they are considered omens. They carry great animal medicine and are to be greatly revered if they come to you in a dream.

Panda

The panda is a powerful symbol of abundance and prosperity. Pandas eat bamboo, long a symbol of luck and good fortune; they also eat it slowly and endlessly, connecting the panda to the concept of never-ending prosperity. Compassion and patience are also energies associated with this beautiful, beloved creature. If the panda should visit your dreams, you are being guided by a very powerful totem.

Shark

The ultimate predator, this is a very common image in a dream that represents fear and anxiety. As a totem, the power of the shark is phenomenal. Sharks represent our capacity to be single-minded, unstoppable, and driven. And yet, when they appear in a dream, they are often feared. When the shark appears in your dream, you must ask yourself what you are afraid of. Such a dream may be calling you to step into your personal power in a bigger way. Focus, self-determinism, and being utterly free of distraction are part of the medicine that the shark has to offer. But first you must get out of the way of your own fears in order to accept such power as your own.

Snake

There is a significant amount of change or transformation in your life if you dream of snakes. Snakes can inspire great and varied personal emotions and therefore can ultimately connect to very different shades of meaning based on your associations. But first and foremost, snakes represent change and transformation. This connects to the fact that they shed their skin in their growth process and that many of them are capable of causing fatality to their predators, implying the symbolic rebirth that follows any death experience. There is a healing element to this, as many snake venoms can also be used as curatives. This may connect to the two snakes that appear on the physician's caduceus, representing the challenge to life and the response of the healer to match it. In the Judeo-Christian tradition, the snake bears the responsibility for tempting Adam and Eve. As such, a snake can represent a confrontation with a change in your value system. It is important to remember that Adam and Eve's yielding introduced the human race to the knowledge of mortality and the birth of consciousness. A serpent in your dream may actually represent a major shift in your awareness that may bring about the death of an old paradigm that brings you into a whole new world. In Eastern cultures, the awakening of spiritual power is often referred to as a snake. Known as kundalini, it is experienced as an incredible energy that undulates up the spine. Stimulating this can induce a tremendous healing force that has the ability to purify the nervous and glandular systems. The practice of yoga is designed to awaken the snake that lies dormant at the base of the spine. As a dream symbol, a snake could represent the potential for power and energy if properly channeled.

Spider

The spider spins a web and then waits patiently for its prey, trusting that all it needs and desires will come to it. In this way, the medicine that the spider carries is of creativity and patience. This is a powerfully feminine symbol. Many, if not most, people have an aversion to spiders, which makes them a creature of the shadow. A spider bite may indicate that an infusion of the feminine principle may be in order for your current dealings to succeed. The irritation, illness, or death that is possible from a spider bite indicates the level of sacrifice that will be required of you on an emotional level at this time.

Tiger

The tiger is the ultimate animal symbol for strength and sensuality and is also connected to vitality and health. When a tiger appears in a dream, you are being acquainted with a powerful totem to guide you through any difficulty. Tiger medicine is the perfect antidote to fear and aversion, for the courage, strength, and cunning associated with this animal are without parallel.

Wolf

One of the most powerful totems associated with the feminine principle, the wolf is a pack animal that is most active at night. This nocturnal behavior connects the wolf symbolically with the shadow and your ability to maneuver in the darker territories of your nature. The wolf's strong association with the moon also cements the relationship between the wolf as a symbol and the moon's connection to cycles, changeability, and all things that relate to the movement of the unconscious mind. When the wolf appears in a dream, you are being guided by very strong forces that know their way around the darker recesses of the psyche.

Apocalypse Dreams

The end of the world is a very common dream image, perhaps more and more so as the world itself becomes more chaotic and frightening. These dreams can take many forms, but most fall into one of two types. The more frequent of these is the impending apocalypse, where the dreamer is certain that the world is about to come to an end and/or there is an imminent threat to the world's survival, such as a nuclear blast or another catastrophe. The other type is the dream that takes place in the post-apocalyptic landscape in the aftermath of such an event.

Change is difficult for human beings. We tend to fear and resist it. And yet the one thing that is absolutely certain in life is that things change, and often quite dramatically. Any death is symbolically connected to the rebirth that is built into it. The same thing is true of the notion of the end of the world as we know it. You cannot have one without the other. It stands to reason that if the world as we know it comes to an end, a new world will emerge as a result of clearing the landscape and everything in it.

An apocalypse dream
tends to come up
when the dreamer is facing
a great deal of change.
It represents the anticipation and fear
that is part of such a moment.
If the dream narrative features
a coming or impending apocalypse,
then the challenge facing the dreamer
is either in the future
or may be a creation of anxiety
and fear of the possibility of change.

An apocalypse dream tends to come up when the dreamer is facing a great deal of change. It represents the anticipation and fear that is part of such a moment. If the dream narrative features a coming or impending apocalypse, then the challenge facing the dreamer is either in the future or may be a creation of anxiety and fear of the possibility of change. If the dream takes place after the world has seemingly come to an end, the dreamer is invited to examine how their circumstances have shifted and consider the difficulties associated with reinventing the self and changing direction in the course of their life. Like all scary dreams, this is one where the sensation of the dream belies the positive message that is buried within it.

Baby

The essential meaning of a baby as a symbol connects to the new life it represents. Babies grow up to become adult human beings, but in their infancy, they embody all the potential that has yet to be expressed. In this way, a baby in a dream is likely to be expressing some new chapter in your life that is just beginning and has yet to unfold into full manifestation. There are intense responsibilities associated with the helplessness of a baby that are key to this particular image. In the dream world, a baby's dependency relates to the fragility of new ideas as they mature into actual life choices and/or options.

Men and women have different relationships to babies that are biologically-based. A woman dreaming of a baby should consider how literally the image may need to be taken. Depending upon life circumstances, there may be issues of concern arising out of parenting or pending childbirth. Additionally, this image in a dream may connect to the unconscious expression of feelings around the ticking of the biological clock, both prior to and moving away from the time frame of fertility. If having a baby is not a realistic proposition in your waking life, there may be elements of wish fulfillment connected to this dream. Also to be considered are frustrations, obstacles, or possible unconscious expressions of futility in whatever creative expression you are currently struggling with.

The same meaning of new beginnings applies to a man having a dream that features a baby as a primary image. The life event inspiring such a dream may require a level of nurturing and attention worthy of this symbol. However, a male dreamer may have to consider the limitations of being biologically unable to create an actual baby as part of an accurate interpretation.

The health of a dream baby might correlate with the vibrancy and strength—or lack thereof—involved in a new venture. Being surprised by the appearance of a baby may equate to sudden changes in direction that are being inspired by new life events. Adoption of a baby could indicate that the new thing in your life may have its origin in someone else's domain. Examine all the information you can remember about the baby and apply what you notice to your interpretation.

Back at School

The primary symbolic meaning for this image is deeply connected to the dream's own personal experience of this period in their life. In a general sense, high school is where most of us learned life lessons of responsibility and sexual identity as well as where we built the foundation for the directions we took as grownups. However, the overall experience of this turbulent time varies from person to person and can range from fun and joyous to excruciatingly painful. When you dream of high school, your unconscious is expressing emotional issues that have their roots in this time in your history.

This common dream is often related to performance anxiety. High school represents the first time that most people face a level of responsibility that is most like what we deal with in the adult world. When our current lives spark insecurity about our readiness to face life's tests, we may express unconscious fears by returning unprepared to this time and suffer the humiliation of being lost, not knowing the schedule, not being ready for an exam, or even finding ourselves naked.

The lessons faced in adolescence were, for some people, accompanied by mistakes being cleared up for us by parents or other authority figures. As such, this dream image could indicate an unconscious wish to have the burden of adult responsibilities magically disappear as if someone else could handle them for us.

If the dream is uncomfortable, look to present stressors that may feel burdensome in the same way you felt as a teenager. The pressure to perform at a certain level is a major theme of the high school experience. This dream may be revealing issues of performance anxiety in your current life. Inherent in this image is the fear of facing the expectations that others may have of you. Examine your current life for issues of this nature and you will be well on your way to an accurate interpretation.

Beach

Ever wonder why so many dreams take place at the beach? It's because this is where, symbolically, the conscious and unconscious minds meet. The ocean represents the deep unconscious mind. Its vastness is mostly hidden from us, just like the unconscious. Land represents our conscious mind, the part of us that is knowable, visible, and open to exploration. Our planet is divided into these two distinctly different surfaces. Where they meet is symbolic of the place in the human mind where what we are conscious of and the depths of that which lies below the surface of our awareness exist side by side. Consider the fact that the ocean covers most of the planet with water, with only relatively small masses of land rising above its surface. The same is true for the human psyche, where most of who we are is unknown to us, hidden in the depths of the unconscious.

As a symbol, a beach can be explored from the perspective of either or both of its two components. The quality of the water connects to your current emotional expression. The land that meets it represents your conscious thoughts. The fact that this is where these distinctly different terrains meet gives this image a mysterious and magical quality, much like our experience of beaches in life. A dream on a beach signifies that new levels of understanding are available to you by virtue of the unconscious and conscious minds communing.

Ceaseless ocean waves exert an enormous impact on the shape, contour, and boundaries of the shorelines that bear the brunt of their constant pounding. The same is true of the mind, which is under a constant barrage of thoughts and feelings that burst out of the unconscious. These thoughts and feelings often spill violently onto the edges of our mind, influencing our moods, behaviors, and choices. This can be experienced positively as creative expression or flashes of insight. However, just like the tides, powerful emotions can feel dangerous, sweeping everything in their wake back into the depths of unknown territory.

What occurs on the beach in your dream, who you are with, the time of day, and all other factors must be examined when interpreting this image. Additionally, your personal associations with the ocean and swimming in deep water is key to an accurate interpretation. Some people thrive in the water and find the act of swimming in the ocean exhilarating. Others feel naturally safe on land and fear deep waters, which can be filled with predators and forceful tides and present the possibility of drowning. There is just as much fear about surrendering to our feelings in our human experience as there is about drowning in the sea. What happens and who appears on a beach in your dreams offers crucial insight into what emotional needs the unconscious wants you to examine.

Being Chased

This is a fairly common dream and certainly is a staple in media-driven representations of the nightmare experience. Countless movies have used this image to dramatize a fear-based response to a threatening moment in life showing up in the sleeping landscape of a character. In some dreams the pursuer is known to the dreamer; other times it is a stranger or simply a menacing force. Sometimes there is one pursuer, while other dreams feature many, in fast pursuit or slowly menacing. Whether the danger is real or the dreamer is making an assumption of danger based on heightened anxiety, this symbol is a staple in the realm of recurring, scary nightmares.

When a person feels exposed on a very primal level, the built-in survival mechanism of the fight-or-flight response occurs. While most people's routine lives do not provide them with chances to test how they would react to such a threat, the dream world is filled with many such opportunities. Being chased is perhaps the most common dream image shared by all people across cultures.

Since being chased is a frequent dream experience yet an infrequent life experience, it is important to recognize that the unconscious mind is using a very intense image to express waking-life stressors that are not as life-threatening as the dreams they provoke. The mind is very economical—it will use the fantastical experience of surviving danger in order to allow us to wake up the next day, ready to face the mundane challenges that may be troubling us. The fact that these are often recurring dreams further illustrates their capacity to balance out the unconscious fears and anxieties that we accumulate during the day. When this dream appears, look to where you may be feeling threatened or anxious in your life.

There is an alternate perspective that is important to consider when dreaming of being chased. Sometimes it is part of human nature to be afraid of success. This unconscious sabotage can be very difficult to identify. You may be running in terror without knowing that the secret enemy you are running from is yourself. If you do not know your assailant, it may simply be you trying to catch up to you with something important that, if embraced, would allow you to feel more complete. If you know who is chasing you, the person may have more to offer you if you let them catch you. Even if being caught ends in being killed, that death could be a symbolic transformation of such significance as to be the very thing needed to bring your greatest heart's desires into reality. That is, of course, if you have the courage to stop running and turn around.

Being Naked

This is one of the most common dream images experienced by almost everyone at some point. It expresses the fear we all have of being vulnerable or exposed in life in a way for which we aren't prepared. In Western culture and especially in the United States, the public is generally not very comfortable with nudity. Given this predisposition to cover up our naked selves, it would be a natural representation in the dream state for nakedness to indicate feeling exposed in some area of life. Where you are naked in a dream and who you are naked in front of will provide you with all the clues you need for an accurate interpretation of such a dream.

Blood

The elixir of life, blood courses through our veins and keeps the body alive and healthy. Lose enough of it and life slips away. If your dream includes receiving or losing blood, this may reflect a message that you are either in need of more energy or are being depleted by some situation. How this occurs in your dream will add texture to your interpretation. A wound inflicted by another may reflect an external struggle, whereas a medical procedure connects more to an internal process necessary for healing.

Science tells us that there are different kinds of blood and that certain types are incompatible with others. In fact, incompatible blood types between a mother and her fetus can be life-threatening. Therefore, dreaming of blood types could connect to conflicts about compatibility that are deeply rooted and may be impacting you in areas of life that you are passionate about. When blood type and compatibility are being examined, the stakes can be as high as life and death. HIV brings a whole new view of blood as potentially dangerous through the nature of the transmission of this disease, effectively shifting our collective-conscious view of blood to a substance to be potentially feared as contagious on a life-threatening level.

Bloodlines have figured prominently throughout history as coveted evidence of ancestry. While this perspective may appear to be an archaic form of class consciousness, we are now aware that blood typology is an effective tool to establish biological ties between family members. If this idea is expressed in your dream, your interpretation should reflect blood as connected to primal feelings about your family connections. Your dream may be expressing this as either powerfully passionate or energetically depleting.

The color of blood is significant in a number of ways. If this is thematic in your dream, your interpretation must examine the meaning behind it. Oxygen-rich and healthy blood has a distinctive deep red color. If tapped out of nutrients, it turns blue. In the world of science fiction, the blood of alien beings can be anything from green to colorless chemical compounds made up of deadly acids.

There are also many culturally based meanings associated with blood. The term "red-blooded" is synonymous with virility and strength. Conversely, to be "blue-blooded" connotes a passivity and lethargy related to wealth or privilege. Issues of racial prejudice often included erroneous beliefs that blood differed significantly between people of

• • • • • • • • • • • • • • • • •

Being naked is one of the
most common dream images experienced
by almost everyone at some point.
Where you are naked in a dream
and who you are naked in front of
will provide you with all the clues
you need for an accurate interpretation
of such a dream.

different cultural backgrounds or skin colors. The mixing of bloodlines was considered by many to be likely to have disastrous results. While that level of ignorance is not as prevalent today as in the past, the foundation of these beliefs still resides in the collective unconscious and is worth considering.

Your personal reaction to blood is also a factor in interpreting this as a dream symbol. Some people are squeamish and find the sight of blood to be very upsetting. For others, curiosity or a sense of eroticism may be stimulated. There are those, too, who are unaffected by the sight of blood because their profession frequently brings them in contact with it. Any of these responses can reveal your relationship to the levels of passion and life force you are currently experiencing.

Celebrities

Just as you might interpret someone in your dreams whom you know based on the qualities or personality traits that they exhibit in waking life, the same process applies to a celebrity, but at a more heightened, aspirational level. Celebrities are the gods and goddesses of modern life and represent archetypal human qualities with which we all identify. The essence of a particular celebrity's image can be distilled into a character aspect by the ways in which we perceive the person. Millions of people hold the same projected image of celebrities. The power of all that magnified perception endows them with superhuman status and removes any sense of the person underneath the persona.

Celebrities show up in our dreams when the stakes are a little higher in terms of what we're dreaming about. By providing a more powerful image, the unconscious is telling you to pay more attention. Approach the interpretation the same way you would anyone in your dreams. When considering the qualities of the person you are dreaming about, remember to look at everything about them and take into account how you perceive them, including if you are a fan or not and whether they are currently in or out of public favor. When interpreting a celebrity from a dream, first consider what they embody on a universal level. Then, and only then, add your personal feelings about them. When you have done this, you will be clear about what character aspect of yourself you are dreaming of.

In the way that people in our dreams represent character aspects of ourselves, celebrities represent character aspects of the global consciousness as reflected by the idea of archetypes. Since celebrities are our modern-day gods and goddesses, dreaming about one of these elite individuals represents a need to explore the qualities they embody as a character aspect but in a much more powerful way. In a process identical to working with a character aspect of an ordinary person, a celebrity's fame elevates the significance of the meaning you assign to them. Your unconscious is using the fame or notoriety associated with their public visibility to get your attention. It is, in effect, providing you with an image that has a chance of making the dream memorable upon waking so that you might more readily take notice of the guidance available to you in the dream.

Sexual dreams with celebrities are common. Most dreamers assume this is so because of how attractive most of them are. Additionally, what they do puts them in a position to inspire the sexual fantasies of the public. However, in dream work, sexual dreams with celebrities are common because the drive to integrate archetypal energy is essential to the evolution of our souls. When the unconscious is encouraging you to own the more powerful parts of your psychic makeup, there is no better way for it to get your attention than through highly charged sexual imagery.

It is natural for us to need larger-than-life representations of the human experience to motivate us to get through the various challenges we face and manage the stressors and disappointments that are a part of life's journey. Our culture's fascination with the lives of celebrities provides us with hope that our own lives have the potential for excitement and glamour, even if this is just a fantasy. In fact, such fantasies can function as survival mechanisms for many people.

The process of discovering what a dream involving a celebrity might be telling you is the same as that with any character aspect. Since we are in the realm of archetypal energy when dealing with celebrities, the quality that your dream is inviting you to explore may be very obvious. A sports figure may be asking you to examine your willingness to play the game of life with more confidence, whereas a pop singer may be suggesting that more self-expression is crying out for release. If you get stuck on how to interpret the meaning of a celebrity's presence, the technique of using three adjectives to describe them works just as well with a famous person as with an ordinary one.

Death and Dying

Death is a powerful symbol of change at a transformational level. All change involves the cycle of something dying to be reborn again. This applies to all of life, from the changing of the seasons to the coming and going of relationships and the process of birth and death itself. Death in a dream signifies that an enormous shift is occurring in your life. An accurate interpretation depends on exploring who died in your dream and how and why it occurred.

Begin with the person who died in your dream. If you know the person from life, decide what character aspect of yourself they are representing. How that person operates in life is what is changing within your own psyche. The change is so great that it is being expressed by the ultimate of changes—death. If the person is a stranger, then use whatever information you can remember about them from the dream to explore what elements of your personality are undergoing a transformation. The quality that is being shifted could be about behaviors, habits, or character traits. It will always be illuminated by the person who dies and what they represent to you. Some dreams of death relate to changing relationships from waking life. Shifting dynamics between people can often feel like a death, and this may be a more literal meaning of such a dream.

The manner of the death can provide additional information to add to your interpretation. The more violent and sudden the death, the more combustive and intense the process you are going through is likely to be. A death that has already occurred could signal that you are in a later phase of change rather than at the beginning. Very often, we are not aware of what needs to be killed off in order for something new to emerge. If your dream offers you very little information to work with, it is very likely that dreams with the same theme will appear in the near future.

Certain people dying in dreams can also reflect specific themes. The death of a parent, for example, could be about needing to let go of ways in which you parent yourself that no longer serve you. The death of a friend could symbolize the letting go of their energetic quality as it lives in you or even a behavior that doesn't serve you that is carried by that person. If it is you who dies, the transformation may be so complete that it involves your entire life or life-style—e.g., moving, changing jobs, a breakup, a new relationship, ending destructive behaviors, etc. Even wonderful new life experiences require a death of the past in order to be fully embraced.

There is an amusing myth that you can never die in a dream, because if you did you would simultaneously die in the real world as well. Obviously this can never truly be substantiated due to the fact that anyone who could actually prove the point would be dead. People do, in fact, have dreams that feature themselves dying. Death is an ending, which must always be followed by a new beginning. This is symbolic and never literal. As a dreamer, trust that you are safe from dying a dream-related death. But, of course, we'll never know for sure.

Some death-related dreams center around funerals. A powerful ritual, a funeral helps people process the death of someone close to them in a collective procedure that acknowledges the loss and marks the beginning of a new chapter in their lives without the deceased. Funerals are often very somber occasions where people feel they have to behave in a certain way that seems appropriately solemn. This restraint can limit the level of authenticity at such events. On the opposite side of the spectrum, there are many cultures in which gregarious expressions of joy are employed to deal with the feelings of grief.

If your dream involves either one of these extremes, consider how a recent life change may be impacting the authenticity of your expression. If your behavior at the funeral in the dream was inappropriately contrary to the expectations of those in attendance, you might want to investigate areas of your life where the expectations of others are causing you difficulty.

In a dream in which you are at a funeral, the identity of the deceased will play an important role in your interpretation. By examining the person as a character aspect of yourself, you can consider what part of your psyche no longer serves you and has been sacrificed. In this case, only half the transformation is complete, because funerals mark a death and not the rebirth that inevitably follows.

A common dream with this symbol involves the dreamer discovering that the funeral they are attending is their own. If this is the case, then the transformation that is taking place is more generalized and may connect to a developmental stage in life or a change of a large-enough magnitude as to imply a death of self. Another potential interpretation of this dream connects to feeling a lack of passion or life force in your current circumstances.

A grave or graveyard connects to death, but with a focus on a connection to the past or a generalized experience of thoughts about death. We humans have a very powerful and profound relationship with our dead. While the bond is ultimately mysterious, there is no getting around the fact that we must stay connected to those who have passed in order to make sense of the present. A graveyard's primary purpose is to provide space for the living to make this connection. In this regard, a graveyard in a dream may be calling you to consider how some element of your current life or some of your personality traits may be the result of generations of family that preceded you.

A secondary symbolic meaning of a graveyard has emerged through the media. A graveyard is also home to all of the dark elements associated with death: ghouls, goblins, vampires, and other creatures of the night. This setting in a dream may be an indication that you are dealing with shadow material as well as the fear of death.

Some dreams simply evoke the idea of death through the powerful image of a coffin. A coffin is made to hold a person after death. As a dream symbol, it should be interpreted by examining the individual inside the coffin as a character aspect of the dreamer. This applies whether you know who is inside the coffin or not. Any death is symbolic of change. When examined as a character aspect, the death represents sacrificing a portion of the personality that is no longer a useful part of the whole. An effective shift requires clearing out old ways of being in order to make way for new, more evolved functioning. Death is always followed by rebirth, but when a coffin is present, it signifies being at the beginning of the transformation process.

If you know the person in the coffin, then considering their personality will tell you what traits of your own are dying away. For example, if the coffin contains a friend or relative who is demanding and overbearing, that very quality may be dying in you or may need to be let go of as a way of behaving in the world. If you don't know the inhabitant of the coffin, you may need to do some investigating in your life about what element of your life needs to change. If the coffin is empty and ready for use, you may not know what is getting ready to be sacrificed in you, but the dream may be a wakeup call to find out. Death in dreams symbolizes change of a powerful magnitude. If any of the trappings of death appear as symbols (such as funerals, urns, etc.), you can be assured that big change is afoot.

Dreaming in Color

Dreaming in color is often viewed as a particular phenomenon that sets a dream apart from others you have. There is an implication here that if a memorable dream is thought of as being vibrantly filled with color, other dreams must be in black and white by comparison. However, all dreams are likely to be experienced with various intensities of color, and the memory of vibrant color is just one more way the unconscious is speaking to you.

Light is experienced as white, but if it is refracted into separate wavelengths, the naked eye can perceive the seven distinct bands of color that make it up. There are also seven energetic centers of the physical body, known as chakras. It is important to note that each of these chakras has a color that is associated with it. The order of the chakras corresponds to the order of the colors as they appear when white light is refracted into its separate vibrations. You can use this information to add texture to the meaning of a symbol if a specific color was indicated in your memory of a dream.

This is only a starting place, as many permutations and personal associations will alter the meaning of colors as you interpret your dreams. However, consider the logic of even some of these distinctions. For example, green is the color of the heart center but is also associated with jealousy or being green with envy. Though these are very different emotions, love and jealousy are both products of the heart. Yellow represents the emotions but has come

Dreaming in color
is often viewed as
a particular phenomenon
that sets a dream apart
from others you have.
There is an implication here
that if a memorable dream
is thought of as being
vibrantly filled with color,
other dreams must be in
black and white by comparison.

to signal caution in the Western world. Again, very different life experiences actually have the same origins when examined closely. It is in paying attention to our gut feelings that we are made aware of when to exhibit caution.

The following guide is meant as a foundation and starting place for symbolic interpretation. In addition to the seven colors in the spectrum, I have also included white and black.

Red

The first color of the spectrum, red is associated with security, grounding, aggression, and passion. This energy is connected with the base of the spine. Often thought of as a color of passion, red aligns with aggression and sexual expression in the masculine principle. We stop at red lights, creating security for ourselves by avoiding the danger of oncoming traffic. Blood is the essence of life force itself and is therefore related to being grounded in the physical body.

Orange

The next color of the spectrum corresponds to the area that is situated near the ovaries in woman and the lower belly in men. Orange is also related to sexuality, but through the feminine principle of intimacy and transformation. It is the color most associated with creativity.

Yellow

Yellow is the color of emotions and gut feelings as well as the solar plexus chakra, creating a relationship with this area of the body and the color of the sun. The solar plexus is where we experience our feelings and the rapid shift from one state to another. Associated with the adrenal glands, yellow connects to adrenaline, the chemical manufactured by the brain that creates anxiety, sudden bursts of energy, and the fight-or-flight response. This is reflected in the use of yellow to indicate caution in signage and traffic management. Of course, many emotional states are very pleasant, which is embodied by our experience of sunlight as warm and comforting. The solar plexus chakra is also associated with self-worth.

Green

Green is the color of the heart center, which can be confusing due to the representation of the heart as red, made especially prominent in Western culture with Valentine's Day. However, green is the central color of the spectrum, and the heart is considered the center of both our physical and emotional bodies. This connects the color green to love, healing, and all matters of the heart. It may be easier to understand the meaning of this color if you consider the earth and Mother Nature's love affair with the color green. Keeping with traffic-signal analogies, if you go when the light is green, that is like following your heart's desire to move forward. When the heart is soured by hurt, green can turn into the menace of envy.

Blue

Blue is the color of communication and connects to the body through the throat and the thyroid gland. There is a connection between our metabolic activity, which is regulated by the thyroid, and the effectiveness of our communication. Through our voice, we communicate with others, but it is through our energy levels that we commune with our immediate environments. Other communication concepts associated with this color are the blueprints that communicate the structure of something not yet created. The call of a hospital emergency is known as a "code blue." Before a brochure or magazine page is printed, the early version used to finalize the design and layout is known as the "blue line." When blood circulation diminishes due to a drop in body temperature, the lips will turn blue and communication will be hindered. These are but a few examples that may not relate to a specific image; however, when the color blue is prominent in your dream, incorporate issues of communication into your interpretation.

Indigo

Indigo is an elusive color—many people would be hard-pressed to describe it or identify it. Since intuition shares some of these same indefinable characteristics, it is ironic that the two are linked. Somewhere between blue and violet, indigo is the sixth color of the spectrum and vibrates with what is known as the *third eye*, the point behind the forehead that is the seat of inner vision. The pineal and pituitary glands correlate with this color, which contains yet another irony: the pineal gland regulates all of our body's rhythmic cycles and the pituitary gland stimulates growth and incites the onset of puberty. They perform these functions at the right and perfect time, as if guided by intuition.

Violet

Violet is the final color of the spectrum and is considered the most spiritual. It is connected to the crown of the head and therefore is not encumbered by the demands of the body. In this way, it is the vibration that is connected to us, but reaches upward into higher realms of energy.

There are many examples of violet (more commonly referred to as purple) being associated with spirituality and high levels of consciousness. Merlin, the wizard from the King Arthur tales, is often depicted as wearing a purple hat. The Purple Heart medal represents the ultimate in bravery. In Catholicism during the holiday of Lent, all images of Christ are covered with purple. People who meditate with discipline report seeing violet light as part of the trance experience.

Black

Though it is thought of as the absence of color to some, in the world of physics, black is actually the presence of all colors in the object that embodies it. It is the color that absorbs the most light, retains heat, and is associated with death, as it is the opposite of life-affirming white. As the color of mourning, black clothing represents the social construct of receiving consolation in some cultures. When we are in mourning, we are surrounded by people who share in our sadness. In the same way that a black shirt will absorb all wavelengths of sunlight, a person in mourning wears black in order to absorb the light from those who surround them. In the world of fashion, black has a connotation of being trendy and sophisticated.

Since nighttime is when blackness reigns, secrecy and the ability to hide are part of this color's symbolic meaning.

White

Purity and wholeness are represented by white, as this is the unification of all the colors of light that are visible to the human eye. For some, white is the color of highest spirituality. For others, it connects to the perfection that arises out of the absence of contamination, as in virginity and chastity. An object that appears white reflects the light outward, absorbing none of the individual colors of the spectrum. It is this concept of reflecting the light that shines onto you back out into the world that embodies the high consciousness associated with the color white

Elevator

A fairly common image that appears in many dreams, an elevator symbolizes the rapid transition between different levels of our conscious and unconscious awareness. In waking life, elevators carry us from one floor to another at the push of a button. The different levels they transport us to connect to various levels of our awareness. We choose our destination on an elevator, aligning this symbol with the choices we make about what areas of our consciousness we are willing to investigate. What happens in the elevator of our dreams may reveal how well this process is going in our daily lives.

The floors involved in an elevator dream can hold significance. In a general way, moving upward connects with higher, more sophisticated levels of thinking and moving downward indicates investigation of lower levels, past issues, and behavior patterns. Moving downward can also align with visiting hidden or shadow material.

The actual floor number or numbers, if remembered, can be examined through the lens of numerology for additional meaning (see *Numbers*). If there are specific associations with the floors you visit or the building where the elevator is located, this should be factored strongly into your interpretation.

To be going up when down is desired may indicate a pressing need to operate with greater insight. Going down when up is anticipated may point to the need to uncover additional material hidden in the lower depths of your consciousness or your past. Being stuck on an elevator is to be midway through a process or shift. Your response to the lack of movement may reveal a level of impatience with your progress in some area of growth.

An elevator out of control is similar to a falling dream, but the added components of transition and choice must be considered. While you may be falling, you have chosen to take the elevator in search of new information. Going sideways is to be confused about the direction in which a current transformational shift may be taking you. If the elevator is out of service, you may be stuck in some area of your life. Another possibility with a broken elevator is a need to stay where you are and not try to escape your current situation by rising above it or sinking to a lower level.

Exes/Breaking Up

This is a very common dream image and often a confounding one. Many people dream of their ex-partners and find the experience disturbing, whether because such dreams elicit grief and sadness or because they are a horrifying reminder of something the person is glad to have in the past. When two people are joined as an intimate couple, the way they identify with each other psychologically is the glue that holds them together. It is almost as if their individual sense of wholeness depends on how each partner lives inside the psyche of the other as a projected "other half." When a breakup occurs, each person moves on to their next expression of self. Neither will ever be quite the same for having connected. Often, dreaming of an ex is a natural part of the separation process that can take years to unfold on the level of the unconscious mind. In other words, dreaming of an ex after the relationship is over is common and perhaps even helpful for moving on.

In a dream, one party (or both, if neither of the two people breaking up is the dreamer) represents a character aspect of the dreamer that is being sacrificed in the cycle of death and rebirth in order to make way for a new way of being. While this can hurt intensely, letting someone go is an intrinsic part of growing and expanding our self-identity as we mature and is a necessary step in the evolution of the human psyche.

Viewed in this light, a breakup in a dream signals that this crucial process is underway. People frequently dream of the partner they have parted with in life while grieving the loss. The symbolic meaning of the ex in a dream connects to the qualities in the dreamer that were most brought out by the ex. If a breakup is occurring to a couple in the dream that is not you, then the character aspects represented by one or both of them will provide clues to the qualities that are being discarded or need to be let go of.

❦

A flying dream
could indicate strong feelings
of freedom and bliss,
which can represent
moving toward a
higher state of awareness
or connection with spirit.

Violence or conflict surrounding a breakup may illuminate an elevated level of resistance or perhaps higher emotional stakes. Consoling someone after a breakup may point to being further along in the process of change. Advising someone or seeking advice around the issue of a breakup could represent an unconscious attempt to battle resistance to change. The varying levels of emotional content in such a dream will reveal the depth of the shift that is taking place.

Dreaming of an ex-partner long after a relationship is over is another challenge to most dreamers. This is because the dreamer is likely to be thinking too literally about the dream's content. The sudden appearance of an ex in a dream years after the relationship ended has nothing to do with the ex. It is a signal for the dreamer to consider the qualities of that person or perhaps the dynamic of that relationship and how they are being triggered by current life events.

Falling

At the heart of it, dreams that involve falling are about a loss of control. Though some falling dreams include a sense of surrender and grace, most are quite terrifying. The fall may be the immediate experience, but what is built into such a moment is not knowing when or how you are going to land. In fact, it is safe to say that it is not the fall that kills you, it is the sudden stop. The real source of the fear associated with this symbol is what may occur and the anxiety about not being able to directly impact the outcome of a situation.

The deeper meaning of falling dreams is that the highest road to take in any difficult situation is to surrender yourself to the lack of control you are experiencing. In any situation where there is no control to be had, letting go is the only powerful choice to make. Most dreams of falling do not end in landing, further cementing the symbolic connection of this image with surrender.

Where and how you land will be directly tied to the quality of your descent. The more graceful the fall, the more likely you will benefit from where you wind up. The context will offer you subtleties of meaning by examining the way you are falling in your dream. Falling backward indicates not being able to see the direction you are taking. Facing forward might enable you to see what you are facing, but your fall still indicates lack of control. Spiral twisting is an even stronger loss, as in spiraling out of control. The amount of fear felt in the dream is the barometer of how much unconscious fear is being suppressed. A fall that is easy and flows with a sense of surrender might be telling you that you are ready to let go of control in some situation. It is also possible that falling in a dream could be a compensatory dream, indicating that some inflation is going on in your waking life. Perhaps you are reaching higher than is appropriate to your current circumstances or level of development.

Flying

Perhaps the most fun you can have while remaining asleep is having a dream that involves flying. This is a fairly common dream, and most people who remember their dreams report having at least one of these in their lifetime. The sensation of flying is so potent that flying dreams often remain with the dreamer for years after having them.

There are several versions of this dream. The gold standard of flying dreams is when you are soaring high above a beautiful landscape, feeling free and expansive. Sometimes the dream is about being able to fly initially and then no longer being able to stay aloft. A very common occurrence is to know that you can fly but only managing to leap up and stay airborne for a short duration. No matter what form a flying dream takes, a satisfying interpretation must take one fundamental element of life on Earth into consideration: gravity and our relationship to it.

When we are born, we move rather suddenly from an underwater world in which we are floating and constantly supported in the closest thing this planet has to offer to a sensation of weightlessness. All of our experiences are informed by this feeling of buoyancy and self-sufficiency. There is no such thing as want; that which we desire in the form of food and sustenance is available before its absence can even trigger an awareness that it is not available. Every need is met and we are simply existing in a metaphorical Garden of Eden.

We are then ripped out of paradise and thrust into a dry and overstimulating world in an abrupt transition from womb to breath. The very first thing we are introduced to is the force of gravity, and very suddenly we encounter the concepts of up and down that were only barely part of our initial experience of our surroundings for the first nine months. As we grow, we eventually begin the laborious process of learning to walk. As we exert the muscles in our core and limbs, we fight against gravity and eventually learn to spend the rest of our lives upright. We learn early on that gravity is a force that must be reckoned with. If we do not respect it, the result will be injury or even death.

There is a waking-life symbolic meaning associated with gravity that must be taken into consideration when interpreting any dream with flying as a key feature, and that is shame. Shame is an emotion that is associated with guilt. It goes deeper than guilt, however, and includes the humiliation attached to feeling as if you have done something wrong. The problem with shame is that it can be caused by criticism and judgment heaped upon you by parents, family members, social circles, and society itself. From the very first time a small child is told no, scolded in some way, or unduly punished, the same cycle begins. It doesn't even take a level of abuse for this to occur; all human beings feel shame. Shame weighs you down, just like gravity.

Flying dreams are about a complete release from shame, fear, limitation, and resistance. This is one of the most common universal dream images. One of the most delightful aspects of dreaming, this cross-cultural symbol means that you are rising above everything that is on the ground. Since this can be a wonderful sensation, it is often associated with intense feelings of a positive nature. A flying dream could indicate strong feelings of freedom and bliss, which can represent moving toward a higher state of awareness or connection with spirit. It can also provide a broader perspective on your life by virtue of giving you a higher vantage point.

However, it should not be overlooked that this very experience can be used as a defense by the unconscious. When a flying dream appears, it begs the following question: Is there anything that is being avoided or overlooked by rising above the conflict or simply not being grounded in reality?

Ghost

A ghost is the memory or imprint of a former idea, concept, or person. Most people consider ghosts in the context of whether they believe in them or not. The argument around their existence is irrelevant in the world of symbols. A ghost is defined as a remnant of a person's energy that remains connected to the physical world after the person has died. Some metaphysicians theorize that a spirit can be stuck here due to unfinished business or an untimely death. There are scientists who explore the possibility of ghosts as bumps in the electromagnetic field of energy that can sometimes be perceived by people who are living. No matter what camp you fall into, a ghost is symbolic of something from your past that continues to have a presence in your consciousness long after the person or event that inspired it has passed. This can include memories, habitual patterns, and even obsessions.

The three things to examine when ghosts appear in a dream is their identity, energetic quality, and intention, if you know it. Who they are will lead you to the part of your personality that is being highlighted by your unconscious. How they appear reveals the power this experience is having on you. What they want will give you clues to the shift your unconscious mind is guiding you to consider.

If the ghost is someone you know who is not actually dead, use the character aspect technique to discover what qualities are traits that you have let go of but that may still arise in your behavior or thought patterns from time to time. Someone who has actually passed away can be considered in the same fashion, but might represent the impact they had on you in life, whether positive or negative.

The influence the ghost in your dream may have can be seen by the form and structure they take. An ethereal and insubstantial energy might point to less of a hold on you than something more grounded and solid. If the dream offers you any clues to the ghost's intention or desire, add that in a literal fashion to expand your interpretation.

In many indigenous cultures, good fortune comes to a dreamer who faces a ghost and doesn't flee. This image in a dream could point to a need to face the ghosts of your past in the form of old choices and behaviors that still haunt you with regret. Accepting the mistakes you made earlier in life is crucial to emotional growth, and the ghosts of your youth will leave you alone when you take on self-forgiveness.

Running from a ghost in fear may represent an unwillingness to face certain inevitabilities. The notion that ghosts are souls who cannot transition to the next level of existence connects with resistance. Consider areas in your life where you are not letting go of something that no longer serves you, or where you are holding on to someone or something that truly may no longer exist in your life in a real way.

Gun

A gun is an image of ultimate power and the desire to exert power over others. Whoever has the gun is in charge. Connected to the masculine principle, the gun represents male-oriented power in an extreme form. The key to understanding this symbol is that the power represented by a gun is available to whoever possesses it at any given moment. Even the most timid individual can wind up controlling any interaction if the intimidating power of a firearm is in their hands.

The masculine principle is related to action and the ability to make things happen. A gun of any type connects to this universal energy, but with an intensity that indicates a lack of balance or containment. While the presence of a gun may imply a sense of control in a chaotic situation, its deadly and unpredictable nature implies a breakdown of stability and the potential for lethal danger.

The type of firearm is important to consider, as this indicates the amount of power being yielded. A handgun relates directly to personal power and should be interpreted as what is available to you as an individual. Something with more firepower, such as an automatic weapon, relates to the ability to express strength on a more social level.

The proximity of the gun in a dream indicates where the power currently resides. Holding the gun puts the dreamer in a position of ownership, but the level of confidence (or lack thereof) should be noted. Having a gun aimed at you indicates that some character aspect of your personality is demanding to be heard and dealt with. If this is the case, your interpretation needs to include working with whoever yielded the gun in your dream. Brandishing a weapon could indicate a need to be seen as powerful in some area of your life. A hidden or concealed gun indicates elusive power that is felt though not flaunted.

Given the role of guns in our culture, how you personally feel about them must figure strongly in how you interpret them as a symbol. The more reticent you are about them, the more power this symbol may have for you. If this is the case, a gun indicates that shadow material is being explored. However, do not be misled into thinking that the firing of all guns in dreams is murderous or even harmful—hunters love their gun like a trumpeter his trumpet. Additionally, something being killed off in a dream can actually be a positive thing, such as an old belief or pattern that no longer suits you.

Being wounded (or wounding someone else) in a dream brings us to the idea of the gun wielding a great deal of power. Where the wounding occurs will provide access to a deeper level of understanding of how this power is impacting you, whether positively or negatively. For example, being shot (or shooting someone) in the chest could be thought of as a destructive act, but it could also indicate the need for your heart to be opened up to receive love. This is especially true if there is a situation in your waking life that involves a level of intimacy that is great enough to be frightening on an unconscious level.

Hidden Figures and Strangers

This archetypal character aspect acts as a messenger from the unconscious mind but is presented as an unknown. The most mundane of this type of figure is simply the stranger, the person in your dream narrative whom you feel you know but who is completely unknown to you in your waking life. At the other end of the spectrum, such a figure can be much more mysterious and often appears cloaked or deliberately hidden from full view. Such a cloaked figure can be an archetypal representation of death or of change and transformation at the most fundamental level.

A hidden or cloaked figure is a powerful archetypal character aspect and a messenger from the unconscious, often thought of as the archetype of death. This image has its essence in anonymity and may therefore never be clearly known to you. As a character aspect, it is a figure from your unconscious mind that has the capacity to visit you in the dream state and deliver a message. The context of the dream will tell you what the message is,

• • • • • • • • • • • • • • • • • •

A ghost is symbolic of
something from your past
that continues to have
a presence in your consciousness
long after the person or event
that inspired it has passed.
This can include memories,
habitual patterns,
and even obsessions.

or at least where to begin looking for it. However, if in your dream the figure closely resembles the commonly held visage of Death—the cloaked figure without a visible face that roams the world snatching the living into the world of the hereafter—then you are definitely experiencing an archetypal dream. This is a dream that is larger in scope than a typical dream and has greater significance in the scope of your life's journey, above and beyond the moment at which such a dream appears.

Deciding whether such a figure is a personal character aspect or the archetype of Death should be based directly on your experience of the dream. If you had the sense that you were in the presence of Death within the context of the dream, your instinct is probably correct. If your dream portends a death, it is almost certain to be a symbolic one, such as the death of an old behavior or relationship in order to make way for something new.

More clarity about whether to consider such a dream as archetypal can be discovered in the structure of the dream itself. Archetypal dreams are usually very simple in their imagery, often having just one setting and rarely containing any spoken words. If your dream was more typical, with shifting perspectives, changes in location, and the exchange of words, then you are in the realm of the personal.

If the dream feels archetypal or somehow bigger in scope than a typical dream, the message may need more time to reveal itself to you. All archetypal dreams connect to the journey toward integration of the self. If the dream feels personal, the context of the dream should offer you clues as to what this hidden or cloaked figure is trying to express. If this is not obvious to you, your work will be to ruminate on what you can glean from the emotional residue of the dream. Eventually your intuition will help you identify the true nature and intention of this figure and of the dream. Perhaps the most important thing to know about such dreams is that they are unlikely to be precognitive and should not be feared as harbingers of tragedy about to befall you in your waking life.

Remember that any person in your dreaming landscape whom you don't know is representing a part of your consciousness. This could be an idea you are having about your life, a pattern of thought or behavior, or an emotional quality that you are either just discovering or needing to call upon to assist you with something that is coming up in your life at the time of the dream. It is not necessary to understand this fully; simply appreciate that fact that your dreams are helping you navigate your current experience and see if more will be revealed in future dreams.

House

A house in a dream is a symbol of the dreamer's sense of self. No matter what other imagery or circumstances may present themselves in a dream, a house is always an unconscious expression of your identity. This applies to any home-like dwelling, such as an apartment, a hotel room, a trailer, a grass hut, or any of the ideas of "home" that exist in the imagination.

The perspective or view of the house takes on a specific meaning. The front of a house connects to your persona, the part of you that you show to the world, while the back of a house is what is private or hidden. What you discover on the inside reflects various compartmentalized aspects of yourself. Side views or alternate angles may be connected to presenting yourself in the world in a limited, partial, or inaccurate fashion.

The size, style, condition, and reflection of abundance levels of the house will play a key role in interpreting this symbol in a dream. You will need to consider the feelings evoked by the house in the dream itself, as well as what comes up for you when comparing it to your actual waking-life home. Whatever shades of meaning you glean from your dream, they must be interpreted as reflecting an unconscious expression of yourself.

A mansion on a grand scale may indicate a sense of your life getting bigger or opening yourself up to greater levels of abundance. Conversely, this could also be revealing a level of inappropriate grandiosity, depending on your current level of self-esteem. A moment in life that feels constraining and steeped in lack might evoke a dream image of a house that is more hovel than home. Yet this same image could be a symbolic representation of a deeper level of humility emerging within you.

A new house might mean a new sense of self is on the horizon, or needs to be. Adding an extension indicates such an expansion may be occurring on a personal level. An older, dilapidated model could represent an outdated view of the self. A house on fire is expressing that powerful levels of transformation are afoot. The details about a house that the dream is offering you should be incorporated into an interpretation of your sense of self at the time of the dream.

If you dream of a specific home from an earlier time in your life, you are looking at the person you are today as a direct result of what was going on back then. This can refer to occurrences in the environment associated with the home and the people in it, as well as developmental issues based on your age at the time.

The rooms in a home also have specific meanings, as described here.

Bathroom

The bathroom is the place of individuation and our relationship with the private self; it is often the first place in a home where, as very young people, we get to shut the door and be by ourselves. Potty training puts a great deal of emphasis on the bathroom as a place where we "make" something, with the focus on the toilet as the only place to do so. In this way, a primal sense of creativity is expressed by dreams that take place in the bathroom or relate directly to feces.

In the innocence of the young, using the toilet is often a public endeavor, celebrated with exuberance. At a certain age, however, a sense of privacy develops, and we use the bathroom as a place to remove ourselves from the influence of others. Add to this the element of shame around bodily functions and nakedness and the bathroom is left with a powerful symbolic meaning that combines the sacredness of the whole, integrated sense of self with the shame of things about ourselves that we wish to hide from others.

Bedroom

The bedroom is the most intimate room in a home, connecting to sleep, dreaming, sexuality, and privacy that we willingly share with others. Sleeping is an act that puts us into our most vulnerable state, so the bedroom can connect to emotional openness and an unguarded state of being. We also keep our modalities of self-expression in the bedroom, such as clothing and jewelry, so dreams in this room are often connected with the preparation for meeting the world with our sense of individual self-expression in tow. Because of its association with the bed and sexual activity, this room symbolically relates to our personal expression of our sexual nature.

Dining Room

Anything related to food and eating connects to our experience of abundance and prosperity. While sustenance is a function of self-care, when the dining room is highlighted in a dream, we are examining our capacity to share what we have with others. As a more public room in a home, the dining room reflects our comfort (or lack thereof) with sharing resources and welcoming others to partake in what we have to offer. Food in such dreams is not always to be taken literally; what we eat or share can symbolically represent resources of energy and time as well as generosity with other elements of life and life's activities. The dining room in a dream also connects to formalities and social customs and your need to either follow them or break free from their constraints.

Foyer

The entryway is the first place other people walk into when they arrive at a home. In this way, the area around the front door is a symbol of what you show to people that may or may not be authentic. Anything that happens in this area of a home in a dream is reflecting the ways in which you are interacting with the world immediately around you, such as your circle of friends or immediate community.

Hallway

If you think of every room in a house as a destination, then the hallway is the transition between them. In this way, hallways are symbolic of choices we make. If you are stuck in a hallway, your dream may be reflecting the process of finding some clarity in a circumstance that is still out of your reach.

Kitchen

This is the heart and hearth of the home, the room where everyone hangs out at a party. The kitchen is where warmth and sustenance are kept. In the same way that the heart and lungs warm and feed the blood in the body, the kitchen does the same for our consciousness. Everything and everyone must, at some point, pass through this room to be fed and nurtured. Dreams that take place in a kitchen are particularly important to pay attention to. They reflect our spiritual and emotional fitness, our ability to administer self-care and still have enough to give to others. If a dream takes place in the kitchen, your interpretation should reflect an understanding of the dream as an indicator of the state of your heart's desires.

Living Room

The most public room in the home, the living room represents the aspects of self that are already integrated and are part of your sense of identity. When we are in the living room in our dreams, we are in aspects of self that are completely comfortable both personally and interpersonally. Your experience of your social identity

It is common to dream
of having sex with people
with whom you would never
ordinarily do so
or even think of doing so,
such as co-workers,
family members,
or acquaintances.

is reflected in anything that happens in the living room of your dreams.

Mountains

If the ocean represents the unconscious mind, then land is the symbolic correlation to the conscious mind. In this way, mountains represent newer ideas, constructs, or choices. They can also represent challenges or obstacles that you must surmount in your life.

Mountains are formed when two opposing vectors of movement in the earth's crust push against each other and rise upward to form a new land mass. Therefore, the mountain is symbolic of the newly formed, high vantage place that rises up out of conflict and confrontation. Remember that changes on our planet's surface first begin in the combustible core below. This relates them to the passion, aggression, and other friction-causing emotional states that occur in the lower depths of the unconscious that, in the long run, build new, higher terrain upon which you can see more of your life.

A person on or near a mountain may be filled with a need to conquer it, as in climbing Mount Everest just because "it is there." Given this, an obstacle or challenge that arises out of opposing forces and is generated by deeper conflicts is what your dream mountain describes. What you do with or on the mountain and how you feel about it is the next level of interpretation.

If you are resting in a peaceful mountain setting, consider that you are in a place of regeneration after a transformation that may have been created by a previously challenging time. Looking at the view from the peak indicates a higher vantage point from which to see the consequences of your inner conflict and where to go next. Climbing up is to be facing the challenges ahead of you, whereas climbing down, though easier, connects to the aftermath of conflicts that have already been solved. The upward climber must remember that, once at the top, they have completed only half the journey.

Parking and Garages

So many dreams contain cars and driving as images. The symbolic meaning of these is, of course, connected to how we are moving about in our lives.

A garage is a symbol for a temporary stopping point in your journey with the anticipation of movement in life. The primary purpose of a garage is to keep one's car safe and protected when not in use. The car is symbolic of how we maneuver through our lives. When a garage is prominent in a dream, some element of how you are moving forward (or not) is being expressed. The essence of a garage connects to being prepared to move out into the world.

If the garage is a private one that is part of a home, then you must use the symbolic sensibility of the house as self to come to a satisfying interpretation. Every room in a home connects to some part of your sense of self. The use or purpose of the room is what illuminates the meaning that should be assigned to it.

The garage represents your potential for movement and direction. If there is a car or other vehicle in the garage, a dream that takes place there may be indicating that there is about to be some movement in a new direction in your life. If the garage is being used for some purpose other than storing a vehicle, consider that your ability to move more effectively in a specific direction in life may be hampered by choices you have made that are taking you away from your intended goals. Are you being distracted from your life purpose in some way?

A public garage indicates that the dream is reflecting issues that center around your social experience. Since there are many cars being stored in such a setting, it reflects a significant number of choices available to you.

Being unable to locate your car in a garage is indicative of being temporarily stuck in some area of your life. Ask yourself where you would like to be heading and what you have to do to prepare yourself for the journey.

Sexual Dreams

Sex is a powerful drive in the human experience driven by hormones, neurotransmitters, and physiological needs. It is increased by the psychological components of desire, intimacy, and fantasy. Between the body's ambition to be sexual and the likelihood of sex itself to be part of the waking-life experience, it is certainly true that sex will sometimes appear in dreams as a literal expression. In other words, there are times when sex in a dream is about sex, but that is the exception rather than the rule.

The essence of sexual intercourse is the joining of two individuals in a process that allows them to be as close to each other as the human body will allow. This translates into the concept of integration as the symbolic meaning of sex. Additionally, the potential for this act to result in the creation of a third entity reinforces this definition. If you remove all sense of eroticism, embarrassment, shame, or titillation, the purity of this symbol is profound. Any characters that appear in a dream engaged in sexual intercourse are expressing an unconscious desire to merge the character aspects of personality of the individuals involved.

If you are participating in sex in a dream, the focus of your investigation will be on your dream partner. The character aspects that person represents are the qualities that your unconscious is expressing a need to integrate into your present level of functioning. These qualities will be easier to identify when you know the person from your waking life; however, this can also be the very element that makes examining such a dream uncomfortable. It is common to dream of having sex with people with whom you would never ordinarily do so or even think of doing so, such as co-workers, family members, or acquaintances.

Oral sex brings an interpretive distinction of relating to communication and the power, or lack thereof, of the dreamer's sense of their own voice. If you are orally pleasuring a penis, you may be appreciating and experiencing a need to take more aggressive power into your speech. To be orally pleasuring a woman's genitalia means that the receptive, sensitive, or creative elements of your personality want to be recognized and embraced. The active position indicates a higher level of urgency than if you are the recipient. If taking on new ways of communicating can be seen as an ongoing process, receiving oral pleasure connects more to the beginning of that process, while giving it might be associated with the end.

The receiving of oral pleasure can often be viewed through the lens of a power differential. The person receiving the pleasure appears to be in power and the person giving it seems to be in a more subservient position. While this is ultimately illusory, a dream featuring this type of sexual scenario may be describing issues of power and authority as opposed to anything that has to do with sex or sexuality.

The object of your affection will give you a great deal of clarity on the matter at hand. This is where many people are disturbed or even horrified by sexual content, for many dreams have us partnering with people from our life with whom we would not ordinarily have sex. However, to the unconscious mind, sex is a symbolic expression of union and has none of the societal or personal stigma we may attach to it. If the person is known to you, use their character aspects to indicate what qualities you are integrating into your communication. If the person is a stranger, use whatever information you can recall from the dream to inform your investigation.

This topic is so sensitive that it may require some specific examples of how to work with sexual imagery. For example, an authoritative boss might feel like an overbearing personality to deal with in life, but integrating such a person as a character aspect transforms that quality into an appropriate level of personal power. A harshly critical and negative personality may actually provide you with a much-needed sense of discernment or objectivity when incorporated into your life. A person who is so childish in their behavior as to be annoying in your waking world can be transformed into a new relationship with your inner sense of playfulness and joy. That arrogant and insufferable person you know may be providing you with a new level of confidence. Such is the power of the symbol of integration as represented by the act of sex.

If you are witnessing others having sex in your dream, the same approach should be taken, but the process that is occurring is less about integrating new aspects as it is about exploring what existing skills you have that may be necessary for you to call upon to face some situation in your current life. Sexual dreams with a partner of the same gender may be asking you to explore your sexuality in a more expansive way. Additionally, male homosexual sex may be pointing out a need to expand the masculine principle, which has to do with action and doing. Female homosexual acts may indicate an increase of the feminine principle, which is creative and receptive in nature.

Teeth Falling Out

At the heart of this moderately common recurring dream image is the emotional expression of insecurity. The content of these dreams runs the gamut from teeth that are loose to teeth that are crumbling or falling out of the mouth in seemingly endless fashion. Though these dreams occasionally include pain and bleeding, more often than not the dissolution of the integrity of the teeth is something that just happens without explanation or cause.

Teeth serve three primary functions. They allow us to process our food so we can nurture ourselves, they express joy when revealed in a smile, and they can indicate aggression when exposed in a snarl. All of these things—nurturance, joy, and protection—connect directly to security and well-being. If a person cannot nurture themselves, attract loving connections, and protect themselves from danger, the basic constructs of a secure life are not likely to be available. Without these three important parts of life, fear will prevail. Therefore, when this dream image appears, issues of personal security are at the forefront of your unconscious expression.

There are various levels of intensity associated with this symbol. It can fluctuate from a slightly loose tooth to having all your teeth crumble out of your mouth in a bloody mess. The scale of intensity of the dream will indicate the amount of fear being expressed. Whether it is a general fear of being out of control, looking bad, aging, or some other issue of unmet needs, the appearance of this dream indicates underlying insecurity in some area of your waking life.

The teeth are used for chewing, and this association can indicate a need to "chew on something for a while," as in mulling over a choice or course of action. "Sinking your teeth into something" refers to taking on life wholeheartedly. Losing your teeth in a dream could indicate an inability or unwillingness to do so. Losing our teeth as children is such a powerful rite of passage. On some level, losing your teeth in a dream will connect to the process of growing up, even in adulthood. Any dream involving the mouth may also point to issues around speaking your truth and having a powerful sense of your authentic voice; conflicts of this nature may also spark a dream about losing one's teeth.

Technology

We live in an age of technology, and the devices we use are actually extensions of how we think and communicate. Ultimately, all devices are symbolically connected to our mind, intellect, and thought processes. When we dream of our devices, we are expressing things about how we are thinking or how we are being challenged by the rapidly expanding technology we are constantly being bombarded with. Here are some interpretations of common dream images that relate to our current state of technological advancement.

Cell Phone

Like a small brain that we carry in our pocket, cell phones are representative of instant communication of thought and connection, as well as a kind of telepathic attachment to all the knowledge in the world. Higher thought and a new level of informational connection around the globe are what you are connecting to in a dream that involves your cell phone.

In a matter of a few decades, the relatively new phenomenon of cell phones has become so commonplace as to be taken for granted in the Western world. They provide an instant connection from one person to another, no matter where either party is located. On the mundane level, they represent the accelerating speed of the world in which we live. Symbolically, they embody the concept of what might be called a supraconscious: the connection between human beings across the planet through technology that provides the instantaneous exchange of ideas almost at the speed of thought.

When considering the symbolic meaning of this particular device, one cannot overlook the limitations that are currently part of the experience of using them. Static interference, abrupt disconnections, and accidental dialing are all pitfalls of this technology. If any of these experiences play a role in your dream, your interpretation must include such challenges. If the cell phone itself holds the meaning of instant connection and higher levels of thought, then a frustrating cell phone interaction symbolizes disconnect instead. Static could indicate that communication is blocked and you are feeling misunderstood or are misunderstanding some life event. The stigma attached to cell phones as pretentious could represent a move toward or away from conformity. A cell phone that cannot make a connection could mean your quick-fix thinking may be failing you. A smooth connection could be telling you that the answer to your communication problems is right there in your pocket.

Computer

A computer is structured very much like the human brain. There is an operating system that allows other software programs to run. This is like the network of nerve cells that make up the majority of brain tissue. There is also a hard drive, which stores everything that has ever been inputted into it. This is akin to the neural pathways created by the brain's recording of sensory data it receives in the form of memory and knowledge. There is RAM, or desktop memory, which is like your conscious mind. This includes your daily production of short-term memory that is processed each night when you dream. The process that occurs during REM sleep is much like backing up your computer files for protection on a daily basis.

When a computer features prominently in your dreams, you are considering how your mind is working. The state of affairs in your dream computer may very well be mirroring the state of affairs in your current thought patterns. If you experience a computer crash in your dream, the same overload is likely to be happening in your experience of some chaotic element of life. Backing up your hard drive in

All devices are
symbolically connected to
our mind, intellect, and
thought processes.
When we dream of our devices,
we are expressing things about
how we are thinking or
how we are being challenged
by the rapidly expanding
technology we are constantly
being bombarded with.

a dream may be a signal to retain new information that has recently been integrated into your sense of self. Writing code or installing new software could connect to changing or upgrading your perceptions and thought patterns in life, or a need to do so. A network of more than one computer may point to a life situation that requires interaction with others on an intellectual or academic level.

How readily you understand and comprehend the computer's functioning in your dream will mirror your waking-life ability to think clearly and learn effectively.

Email

Email is the instant communication venue of the new world order. We are simultaneously brought closer together and further isolated by this almost instantaneous way of connecting our thoughts to the minds of other people. The realm of the intellect is represented by this image. The newness of Internet technology imbues the symbolic meaning with a sense of uncharted territory in the world of thought and interpersonal expression. We live in a time where the technology has evolved faster than our ability to formulate a universal sense of etiquette and propriety. Its speed implies spontaneity. However, the ability to edit and alter our words prior to sending the finished product adds a dimension of control that should not be overlooked when arriving at an accurate interpretation.

Words typically account for about 20 percent of any verbal interaction. Absent from the email experience are the crucial elements of tone and body language. Despite this enormous limitation, most people approach emails as if they were clear and accurate when, in fact, they are subject to projection and presumption. In this way, an email in a dream connects to communication that is assumed to be lucid but may not be received with the same intention with which it was sent.

The immediacy of the keyboard allows for an enormous amount of editing. We read as we type and retype as we read, changing our words until we are satisfied with the final product. This can lead to a subtle lack of authenticity and spontaneity that did not exist with handwritten or typed letters. This image invites you to consider what role restraint or manipulation may be playing in your thought process. Writing an email might represent a need to figure something out that needs direct and immediate attention. Anticipating a reply may represent wanting an answer to a question you have.

The person you write to or receive emails from will help you uncover what areas of your psyche need to be interacted with. An email from a supervisor at work might point to a search for inner authority. A reply from a beloved might connect to decisions around romance and relationship that require fast consideration. Junk mail and spam might point to undeveloped thoughts or ideas that are routinely cast aside as worthless. They can also represent a general sense of overwhelm due to sensory input that may not feel important to you.

Transportation

All forms of transportation in dreams connect to the symbolic meaning of movement, change, and transformation in our lives. A journey in waking life begins in one place and culminates in another, and everything is different when we are through. In this way, when we travel in our dreams, we are acting out what happens when we go through something that impacts our growth as human beings. We start out in one place and end up somewhere else. Here are a few ways this can show up in dreams.

Airplane

Any means of transportation in a dream is symbolic of the way we move through our lives. Because of the dramatic way an airplane leaves the ground and speeds you to your destination, it is connected with any sudden transition in life. In a dream, changes of this nature can connect either to something that is taking place in your life at the moment or to one that is needed or wished for. Because a plane is our world's fastest mode of public transportation, it connects symbolically to those moments in life when change is rapid and total.

When dreaming of plane travel, the first consideration is to look to where your waking life is shifting dramatically. When you have identified this, use the rest of the dream images to discover how you are feeling about the change that is afoot. If the movement of the plane makes you very anxious, you might be expressing fear over sudden changes that you perceive to be dangerous. A more relaxed or passive response to a plane in your dreams could indicate a level of acceptance but could also signal issues of avoidance. Be vigilant in your investigation.

Missing your plane could indicate a sense that something is passing you by and may illuminate a need to take stock of how aware you are of the opportunities in your current situation. Being stuck on a plane might connect to feelings of impatience and the need to accept external limitations. A plane crash indicates that something in process may not have been working properly and will have to start over. Take a look at the areas in your life that are stagnant or erupting—you may need to fasten your seat belt and take off.

Boat

This is a dream image that connects specifically with your emotional journey through life. A boat travels over water, the universal symbol for anything that deals with the emotions. The size and type of boat in your dream will illuminate your current ability to navigate emotional issues based on resources and levels of skill. The water itself connects with the nature of the emotional territory in which you currently find yourself. The destination of your trip will offer insight into what may be causing an upsurge of emotion and what you hope the outcome will be if you are successful in arriving at your intended destination.

A slow-moving cruise ship denotes the slow, steady pace of emotional unfolding. However, it travels over the deep waters of the ocean, connecting to a need to exert enormous control over what might be underlying fears about the depths of your emotional unconscious. A speedboat indicates faster processing of emotional turmoil as well as a desire to get through an emotional encounter as quickly as possible. A sailboat connects to the merging of emotion and intellect. The boat itself rides on the water of the emotions, while the sail catches the wind of the intellect and uses that as the power that propels you forward. A canoe might harken back to more primitive emotions. A rowboat indicates that the emotional issues you are facing require direct effort to get through them.

The state the boat is in has great meaning with regard to your effectiveness and the safety of your journey. One that is in disrepair or in danger of sinking indicates overwhelm over your current situation. A boat that is docked represents emotional journeys that are yet to be taken. Consider how protected you feel by the boat. Feelings of danger may indicate resistance about diving into the depths of your unconscious feelings.

Bus

When you ride a bus, you turn the reins of control over to another, take a seat, and go along for the ride. Relinquishing the driver's seat is an important point to examine, as your comfort level in the dream will help deepen your interpretation. Positive reactions to riding a bus may point to the well-being that can accompany letting go of control. A negative experience may point to resistance to such surrender.

Given that most bus rides are associated with public transportation, the symbolic meaning of your dream may connect to paths in your life that you share with others in your community. Consider who else was on your dream bus for clues to what area of your life is being illuminated.

The type of bus offers shades of meaning. A school bus may indicate regression to an earlier mentality, whereas a public transit bus could point to a need to follow a course that requires being patient with the paths of others. A private bus, such as a tour bus, may indicate levels of abundance and the need to gather creative resources for future use. However, if the bus was used in place of a car, feelings of lack and limitation may be indicated. If you were not actually riding the bus in your dream, the meaning you give your interpretation should explore this. If this is a bus you should have been on, you might want to consider what obstacle or resistant thought is keeping you from moving more effectively on your life's path.

Car

Since we rely so much on our automobiles to get where we're going, a car represents the connection we have to our path through life. Its speed, working status, style, etc., represent our feelings about our movement on that path. Any time you dream of a car, your unconscious is expressing thoughts and feelings about where your life is going at that moment. The best interpretation will combine this basic definition with shades of meaning based on other elements of the dream.

For example, an old car may point to an old way of maneuvering, whereas a new car may indicate you are moving through life in a new way. A car from your past indicates that part of your history is under investigation. A fantasy car may symbolize the path you wish you were on. Driving someone else's car might indicate a path that has been abandoned for the sake of another's wishes, or even another's path that you wish to emulate. A parent's car could indicate the path taken by virtue of the wishes of the parents. A dirty car might indicate something that needs to be cleaned up. A crashed car could be calling you to examine the choices you are making on your path through life—are you paying attention to the danger signals?

Driving

Driving in a dream represents your movement on your path in life. As a culture, we are dependent on our cars on a daily basis. They take us where we are going in our lives with such regularity that they hold the symbolic meaning of how we are moving on our path through life. The circumstances around the car and the driving experience will identify for you what emotional and psychic challenges are surrounding you at this time.

If you are driving out of control in the dream, you must consider what area of your life might be beyond your ability to regulate. If you are in the back seat and need to gain control of the car, look for ways in which you haven't yet stepped up to the plate. You may not be able to do so yet because of circumstances beyond your control. If your car isn't responding to you, you may be feeling ineffectual about taking charge of some path you are traversing. Varying speeds might be reflecting movement in life that feels either too fast or too slow for your comfort.

A vehicle other than a car might point to being in foreign territory. You may not be feeling confident in your ability to work with the circumstances you have been handed. Causing an accident could be inviting you to look at the consequences of your choices. Being a victim of an accident might encourage you to look at the ways in which you have abandoned your own direction because

• • • • • • • • • • • • • • • •

All forms of transportation
in dreams connect to
the symbolic meaning of movement,
change, and transformation in our lives.
When we travel in our dreams,
we are acting out what happens
when we go through something
that impacts our growth as
human beings. We start out
in one place and
end up somewhere else.

of another person or outside force beyond your control. Driving in the rain connects emotional issues to your current route. Icy conditions indicate that emotions are being frozen over, making your way treacherous. Driving down or up a hill would illustrate the sense of effort or ease involved in your life movement.

Road

The road in your dream is a symbol of your path or direction in life. Your individual path is a combination of past choices you have made and current circumstances and decisions you are about to make that determine the road you're on in any given moment. Such an image in a dream is representative of your current life path. It can be a snapshot of where you are and how you feel about the present moment in your journey.

The context of the dream will offer you the foundation for your interpretation; however, the type of road and its environment will give you deeper shades of meaning. The more isolated the road, the more the dream relates to your private life and personal issues. A public or widely traveled road will likely connect to aspects of your life that are more social in nature.

If the vehicles in your dream are traveling fast enough to inspire anxiety, you may be expressing a fear of being able to match the speed of life around you. Heavy traffic that slows you down may indicate feelings of frustration with the pace of your life and the presence of obligations and responsibilities. If the road is straight and smooth, you are probably moving along comfortably toward your goals, whereas if it is bumpy or treacherous, you may be complicating your journey in some way. The sophistication of your vehicle (from feet to sports cars) may mirror the skills you have at your disposal.

If you know where you are heading, the interpretation you attach to the road will inform you of your feelings about your destination and the process involved to get there. Not knowing where you are going is not the same as having no destination. The former implies ignorance, while the latter could indicate a moment of surrender. Being on the wrong side of the road going against traffic could be mirroring resistance you are meeting in your life.

Train

Traveling by train connects to elements of life that are more social and shared at a community level. Train travel is a throwback to earlier times, and there is a sense of romanticism about it. If this is the type of experience that appears in your dream, you may be considering a nostalgic connection to the past or a more romantic approach to your journey through life.

On the other side of the same coin is the notion of high-speed rail, which is very modern and growing in scope on the planet at this time. The context of your dream will help guide your interpretation. If you are traveling on a train that reflects this new, powerful technology, you may be imagining a speed of transition or change that is not quite available to you.

Subways or other urban rail systems are about making connections in a very dense landscape. You can think of a cityscape as akin to a constellation of thoughts, like ideas that are so massive in your consciousness it takes an entire city to represent them. The chaos of a city is much like the chaos of your mind. It takes an underground train to navigate such terrain. A dream inside a subway train may be pointing to a need to make sense of a great deal of information in a simple and distilled sort of way.

Trains have a very interesting relationship with the tracks they run on. Unlike all other modes of transportation, the routes they follow are laid down in a rigid and specific pattern. Any diversion from this mapped-out way of proceeding could result in absolute calamity. In this way, any dream that includes a derailed train or a crash involving another train on the same tracks needs to be considered from the perspective of the dreamer's relationship with rules, old habits and patterns, and the ways in which we are expected to move about the world. Your dream of a crashing train may indicate a moment when following the established way is interfering with your true authentic expression.

Water

Water is symbolic of the emotions. On a biological level, this is so because of the connection between emotional expression and tears. The human body is made up primarily of water held together by protein-based structures. When we cry, we lose some of that water in a stream emanating from the eyes. While we do not really understand why we cry, we do so when we are deeply moved. This mysterious leakage of precious water is akin to the feelings of loss that accompany it.

If all water is viewed as a symbolic representation of emotions, both conscious and unconscious, then it is the form the water takes in your dreams that will inform you of the size and scope of the expression being illuminated by your dream.

As a general rule, weather-related water connects to conscious emotional expression and flow, whereas bodies of water contain some element of that which is unconscious. Rain and storms occur in the atmosphere and often over land, which represents the emotional content of the conscious mind. When large portions of water are only partially visible, that which is below the surface and unseen is symbolic of the powerful hidden emotions of the unconscious mind. When water is contained in any way, the dreamer's impulse to control some element of their emotional nature is being expressed.

Violent movement of water, such as rapids, waves, riptides, and storms, represents the overwhelming power of emotional material. Your response to such images in a dream is indicative of your level of fear and resistance, or your lack thereof. Lying near water may reflect being close to a willingness to explore the emotional territory outlined by the dream.

Being thirsty and/or drinking water could indicate a strong need to take more emotional sustenance into your life. Drowning might indicate an overwhelming level of unmanageable emotion or the fear that any emotional outpouring might result in suffocation. A waterfall represents the way feelings can cascade down upon us suddenly and with great force, which can be both sensual and exhilarating or painful and overwhelming. Using water to clean (anything from laundry to personal grooming) could indicate the need for emotional healing through working directly with your emotional issues.

Weather

All dream scenes can be considered both as macrocosms and microcosms of your life. The settings of your dreams are, in any given moment, a snapshot of your own consciousness. For example, if you dream of a home, the house, apartment, or room that you are dreaming of is a reflection of some aspect of your consciousness at the time you have the dream. This same principle applies to every dream setting. In this way, the weather of your dreams—if that is a featured image within a dream—could be considered the emotional expression of the dream landscape itself.

Water is always a symbolic expression of emotion. Since falling rain is very similar to tears, rain is the closest representation to the act of crying. As such, it symbolizes the process of allowing our feelings to flow freely. Rain is considered cleansing, for it washes away dirt particles and leaves the air clearer. Tears can also be said to wash debris from the soul. Rain in a dream indicates that an emotional experience is taking place that is ultimately healing. The context of the dream will offer clues to what area of your life is evoking such a deep emotional response. Your reactions to the rain as well as the quality of the rain itself will provide even more information for your exploration.

A light, gentle rain could indicate a small disruption in your life that is causing some emotional reactivity. Torrential downpours, such as hurricanes, point to more intense undercurrents of feeling being expressed. The relative intensity of the rain in your dream will mirror the intensity of what your unconscious is trying to express. How you respond to the rain in your dream will illuminate for you the level of resistance you are in. The mightier your attempts to escape the onslaught of the downpour, the more likely you are avoiding the free flow of emotional expression.

Wind, on the other hand, is the mental and intellectual equivalent of planetary expression. The wind is like the constant flow of thoughts and ideas in our minds. If you think of the earth as the collective consciousness of all the beings that live on it, the wind would be akin to the ceaseless flow of information that passes through our heads. We may not always be aware of it, but it is a constant force to which we are forever adjusting. It is only when the wind changes suddenly that we tend to notice it. It can vary in intensity, from a pleasant breeze to a howling gust. However, like all forms of weather, the wind never stops and it blows where it wants, without any concern for how we feel about which way it is moving.

Air represents the intellect, so its movement is symbolic of the direction of our thinking. Like the wind, thoughts often flow through our minds in a way that seems unstoppable. These thoughts can push us in certain directions in life. Sometimes we go with the flow, whereas other times we resist and push ourselves against the direction in which the winds of thought are blowing. Since we all experience the same wind at any given moment, what becomes important to notice is your individual response to it. A gentle breeze could be either pleasant or uncomfortable depending on the temperature. Dramatic gusts can be exciting for some people, while others may find them maddening.

The behavior of the wind in your dream and your response to it will provide you with an accurate interpretation. The strength of the wind is indicative of the degree of power some life circumstance is exerting over you. Your movement with regard to the wind's direction will illuminate whether you are being supported in your choices or meeting with resistance. A constant wind could mean there is an obsessive thought pattern running through your mind. This can be very creative when they are affirmative thoughts of creative manifestation. However, compulsive obsession is one of the most destructive activities the mind can engage in. It can take your life in directions that don't serve you. The more fear that is present in the dream, the more likely you are facing something that needs your attention. Identify what life situation is in the process of shifting. The winds of change are powerful and unpredictable. Your dream may be an assessment of how you are responding to the things you cannot control.

Extremes of weather experiences, such as thunder and lightning, represent similar extremes with regard to emotional expression gone wild. Lighting is symbolic of sudden awareness or enlightenment born of divergent, confronting ideas. Like a flash of awareness, lighting can illuminate the dark of night, and for a moment everything is clear and visible. Thunder is the booming announcement of the shift or change that is part of the awakening that is represented by this phenomenon. When either thunder or lightning appear in a dream, you may be responding to a paradigm shift or sudden awareness that has just occurred or needs to occur in your waking life.

A tornado is a destructive force of opposing energies. These weather phenomena are incredibly destructive and completely unpredictable in their movement. The devastation they leave in their wake is almost unfathomable, but there is also an element of creation, as their symbolic meaning lies in their formation. A tornado is the result of two air masses of very different temperatures colliding with each other. Under the right conditions, these two systems meet up with each other and each tries to force the other to submit to their direction of movement. As a result of this conflict, the two form a third energetic system, which combines the force of both, creating a tornado.

Resistance is at the essence of the interpretation of this image, so look for areas in your life where you may be in resistance when a tornado appears in a dream. In addition, the chaotic nature of a tornado's path makes this a perfect expression of waking-life chaos. This dream may be indicating an unconscious reaction to the unpredictable nature of how things are unfolding around you, especially in areas where you are facing direct opposition to your desires.

Of course, not every dream that you have can be interpreted with the archetypes in this chapter. However, you have hopefully seen by now the way in which universal meaning works. When in doubt, simply consider one dream image at a time. Ask yourself, what does this thing do? What is its purpose? If it is a person or an animal, consider its qualities. When you approach your interpretation process through the lens that every image in a dream is reflecting some part of you and your personality, it becomes possible to have a deeper understanding of all the elements of your ever-expanding sense of self.

IN CONCLUSION

I had a dream. I have a dream. Ever notice how we use the same phrase to describe both the nighttime phenomena where our imagination rules and also the daytime musings of a magnificent waking life? In dreams, anything can happen and probably will. We trust that and never question the powerful creative force that we find in that mysterious landscape. Well, life can be like that too when we trust the same principles to guide us—imagination, the power to create anything, and the willingness to go with the surprises and unexpected shifts that make life so interesting. My belief is that when we live our waking life more like it is a dream, we can be happier and more excited by what is possible. This is why I am so devoted to helping others look at their dreams with more curiosity and devotion.

There is a wonderful story that is told in many different circles. It tells of a dreamer having an awful nightmare in which they are being chased by a cloaked figure. During the course of the dream, the assailant becomes more and more menacing, finally cornering the frightened dreamer up against a wall. In abject terror, the dreamer cries out to their nemesis, "What are you going to do to me?" After a moment, the dark and menacing figure simply replies, "I don't know. It's your dream!"

By now you should have a better sense of what dreams are, why we have them, and what to do with them in order to understand them better. Of course, the scientific approach may leave you wanting. Are dreams meaningful visits to the more mystical realms of the human experience, or are they just the random, chaotic result of brain cells firing off while important brain processes are happening? Only you can decide for yourself. Hopefully, this *Little Book of Dreams* has helped.

INDEX

Acknowledgments

It is a beautiful privilege that people share their dreams with me. Dreams are so very intimate, and when I hear someone's dream, it is like being invited for a tiny glimpse of their soul. I want to take a moment to thank several people specifically for their contribution to this book: Krista Aventura-Nerestant, Blaire Chandler, Mary D'Agostino, Nick Silber, and Mahla Strohmeier.